how to
construct built-in and sectional
BOOKCASES

Donald R. Brann

Library of Congress Card No. 67–27731

NINTH PRINTING — 1976
REVISED EDITION

Published by
DIRECTIONS SIMPLIFIED, INC.

Division of
**EASI-BILD PATTERN CO., INC.
Briarcliff Manor, NY 10510**

NOTE
Due to the variance in quality and availability of many materials and products, always follow directions a manufacturer and/or retailer offers. Unless products are used exactly as the manufacturer specifies, its warranty can be voided. While the author mentions certain products by trade name, no endorsement or end use guarantee is implied. In every case the author suggests end uses as specified by the manufacturer prior to publication.

Since manufacturers frequently change ingredients or formula and/or introduce new and improved products, or fail to distribute in certain areas, trade names are mentioned to help the reader zero in on products of comparable quality and end use.   The Publisher

Allow Fate to Lend a Helping Hand

Ever notice what strange ways some people "strike it rich." A destitute miner drops off a slow moving freight and discovers a gold mine. Treasure hunters discover sunken ships containing millions of dollars worth of Spanish bullion because a storm, and a drunken employee, prevented their reaching a previously scheduled exploration site. Because I couldn't afford to cut the wrong length, luck smiled on me when I applied the concept of a dress pattern to lumber. And so it goes, everyone is given great opportunities if they give fate a helping hand.

While no one really knows what the future holds, most good luck stems from one single source — problems. These are fate's hand maidens. Every problem you solve creates stimuli that power forward movement. Every step forward creates new and larger problems. Accept each as a step up the stairs to good fortune, and you soon sit in the sunshine of success.

The biography of every important person is woven with the same golden thread. Each continually attempted doing something they had never done before. Without fully recognizing the process, each lived comparable lives filled with doing.

When you realize a minute today is worth an hour tomorrow, and invest these precious minutes in constructive effort, fate lends a hand.

Don R. Brann

TABLE OF CONTENTS

Handsome Bookcases Begin Here...

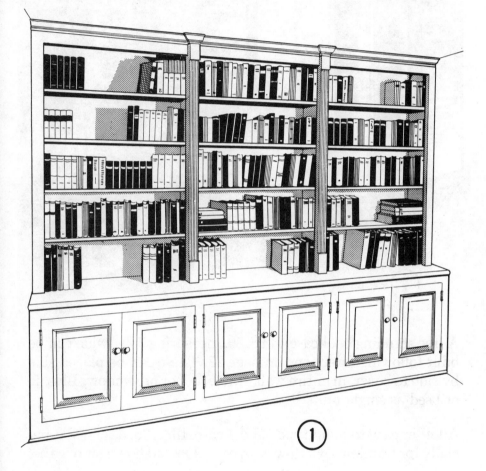

Building a wall-to-wall bookcase, Illus. 1, isn't difficult, nor need it be expensive. Since it adds great charm and convenience, you increase the value of your house an amount far exceeding the price you pay for materials or even some custom-built installations. Step-by-step directions explain how to build any length, depth and height space permits.

②

A free standing bookcase, Illus. 30, measuring 35½″ wide can be built following directions on page 28. These can be placed side by side to cover an entire wall, frame a door or window, Illus. 2, or used as single units.

Another easy to build type of bookcase, Illus. 75, designed especially for framing a window, mirror or door, is shown on page 56.

Read directions through completely before buying materials. Note location of each part in each illustration when same is mentioned.

The list of materials specifies stock lumber best suited for each part. If you decide to alter height, depth or length, use lumber, plywood or flakeboard to size required.

For greater strength and rigidity apply glue to all permanent wood-to-wood contacts.

Always check ends of lumber with a square, Illus. 3, before measuring and cutting to length required.

Always use a square when drawing a line.

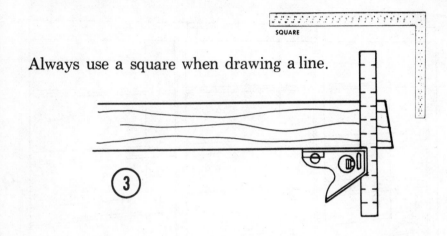

SQUARE

③

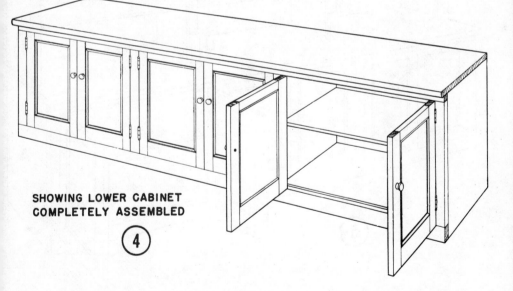

SHOWING LOWER CABINET
COMPLETELY ASSEMBLED

④

While the wall-to-wall installation shown in Illus. 1, has the appearance of a built-in unit, it doesn't have to be nailed to ceiling or wall. Directions explain how to build it in two sections, a base Illus. 4; a shelf section, Illus. 5.

If you want to cut end A and top Q out of one piece of plywood for a one piece unit, it's OK. We recommend the two part construction because it's easier to handle.

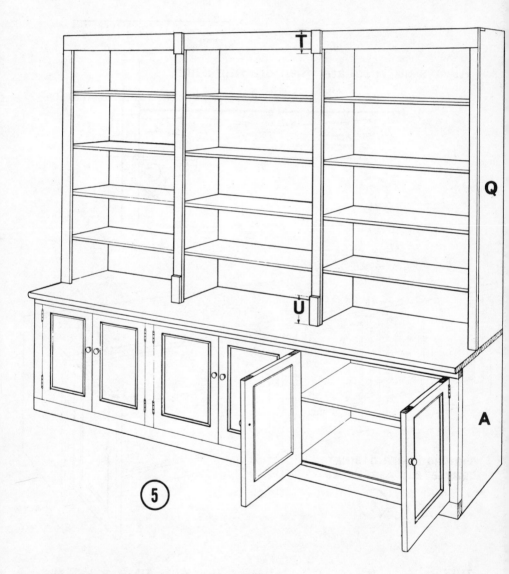

LIST OF MATERIALS

Materials suggested are ample for a 12'0" bookcase, 8'0" high. Always order lumber as listed and you'll make lumber dealers very happy. 1x2 — 4/12, 2/8 means — 4 pcs. 1x2x12', 2 pcs. 1x2x8'.

1x2 — 4/12, 2/8
1x3 — 4/12, 1/8
1x6 — 1/12, 1/14
1x8 — 5/12, 1/8 or use 3/4x4x8 plywood good two sides
1x10 — 6/12
1x12 — 1/14
5/4x3 — 3/12, 1/10, 1/8
5/4x4 — 1/12, 1/10
1 — 3/8 x 4 x 6
36 lineal ft. ¼" quarter round
36 lineal ft. 3/8 x 1/2 stile or glass bead
14 lineal ft. 1 ¾ x 2" crown moulding or use EB #19
   hardwood molding
10 lineal ft. ¾ x 2¼ Pilaster molding
12 lineal ft. BW111 ¾" molding
1 box 1" brads
1 box ⅜" corrugated fasteners
1 lb. 4 penny finishing nails
1 lb. 6 penny finishing nails
1 doz. 2" #12 screws
9 doz. 1¼" #9 screws
50 lineal ft. of metal shelf standard
6 pairs 2½ x 1¹¹⁄₁₆ loose pin butt hinges
6 bullet type cabinet door catches
6 1" or 1¼" door knobs or pulls

Due to the variation in lumber width and thickness, consider stock lumber as measuring:

1x2 — ¾ x 1½"   1x12 — ¾ x 11¼"
1x6 — ¾ x 5½"   5/4 x 3 — 1¹⁄₁₆ x 2½"
1x8 — ¾ x 7¼"   5/4 x 4 — 1¹⁄₁₆ x 3½"
1x10 — ¾ x 9¼"

5/4" stock surfaced four sides, (S4S) will measure 1¹⁄₁₆" to 1⅛" thick. Plywood and flakeboard measures full thickness specified.

If bookcase is to be painted, use ¾" flakeboard, or ¾" fir plywood, good two sides. This means both faces will be sanded smooth.

If you want to build a prefinished hardwood plywood (or flakeboard) bookcase, using walnut, cherry, or other hardwood, ¾" thick veneered panels are available on special order. Since these are rather expensive, you can achieve the same effect, at considerably less cost, by gluing ¼" prefinished hardwood plywood to ½" fir plywood or flakeboard, Illus. 6. The edge can be finished with paper thin matching wood veneer.

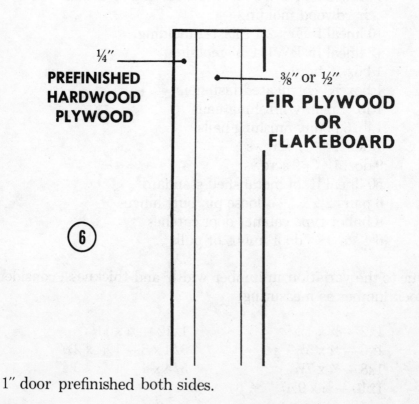

¼"

PREFINISHED HARDWOOD PLYWOOD

⅜" or ½"

FIR PLYWOOD OR FLAKEBOARD

⑥

1" door prefinished both sides.

TOOLS NEEDED

You will need a hammer, cross cut, rip and coping saw, plane, carpenter's square, combination square, chalk line, plumb bob, level, nailset, folding rule and screwdriver, Illus. 7. A chalk line simplifies marking straight lines on floor, wall or ceiling. You merely apply chalk to a line, stretch it between two points, hold taut against surface, snap, and you have a straight line.

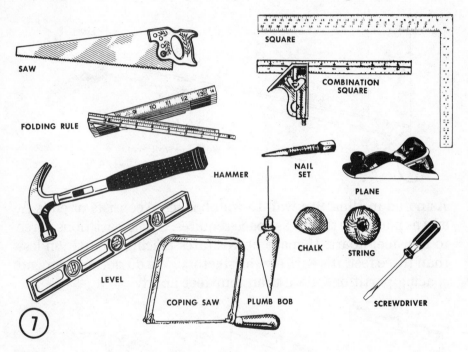

WALL TO WALL BOOKCASE

To simplify construction and to build like a "pro," the shoe, base and ceiling molding within area of bookcase, Illus. 8, should be removed.

Measure 16¼″ from back wall. Snap a chalk line on ceiling. Drop a plumb bob from ceiling line to floor. Snap a chalk line on floor. Now measure distance from line on floor to wall — not to baseboard. If it measure 16¼″ or more it's OK. If it measures less than 16¼″, move floor line to 16¼″, snap a new line. Using plumb bob to guide you, snap a line on ceiling plumb with new line on floor.

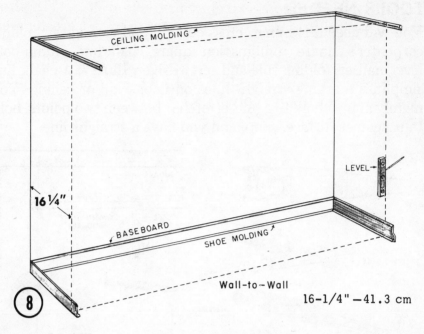

CEILING MOLDING

LEVEL

16 ¼"

BASEBOARD

SHOE MOLDING

Wall-to-Wall

⑧

16-1/4" —41.3 cm

As noted in Illus. 9, a wall-to-wall bookcase consists of ends A, and as many partitions as space requires. Space partitions three to four feet apart. If space necessitates placing a partition less than three feet, it's entirely satisfactory. We do not recommend spacing partitions more than four feet apart.

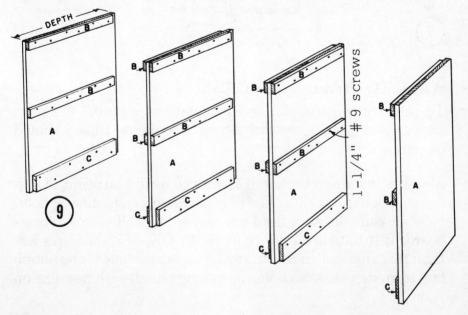

DEPTH

B

B

A

C

B

B

B

A

C

B

B

B

A

C

1-1/4" # 9 screws

B

B

A

C

⑨

Step-by-step directions explain construction of a 12′ built-in unit. Alter length of material if you want to cover a greater area.

Cut ends A-15 x 29¼″, Illus. 10. Use ¾″ plywood. Cut twelve 1 x 2 x 14¼″ for B. Cut six pieces of 1 x 3 x 13½″ for C. (B and C can also be cut from ¾″ plywood.)

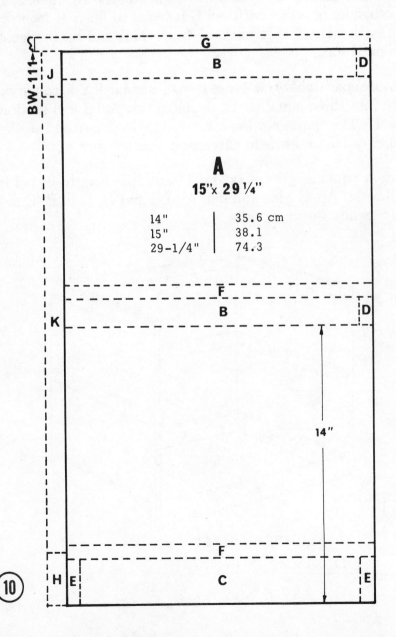

14″	35.6 cm
15″	38.1
29-1/4″	74.3

Apply glue and fasten B to inside of A, in position indicated, Illus. 10. Fasten C to A, ¾″ from front and back edge of A to allow for E.

Fasten with 1¼″ No. 9 screws.

Apply glue and fasten B and C, in position shown, Illus. 9, 10, to both sides of each partition. B is fastened flush at front, ¾″ from back edge. C sets back ¾″ from front and back edge on each partition.

Measure space where bookcase is to be installed. You can divide space into three equal parts, or make two equal end sections, Illus. 11. The center section can be equal in size to end section, smaller or larger, as taste and space dictate.

Cut four equal lengths of 1x2 for D, and four lengths of 1x3 for E, Illus. 11. Apply glue and nail A to E and D, D to B, E to C with 6 penny finishing nails.

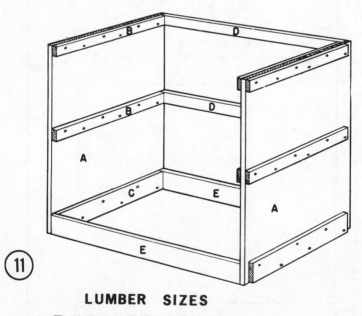

LUMBER SIZES

D − 1 x 2 S4S to ¾ x 1½″

E − 1 x 3 S4S to ¾ x 2½″

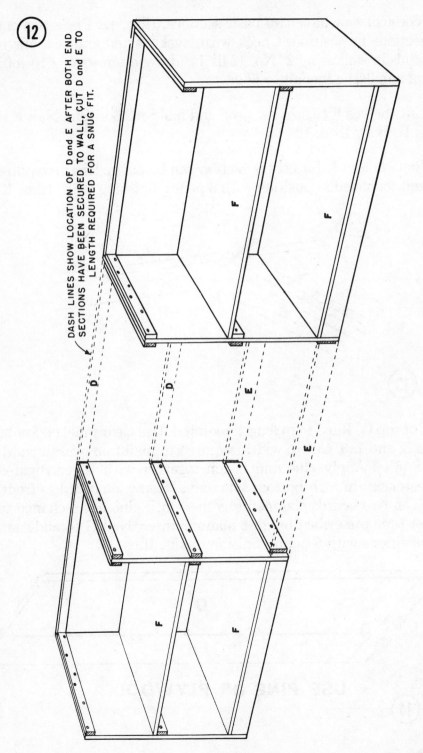

DASH LINES SHOW LOCATION OF D and E AFTER BOTH END SECTIONS HAVE BEEN SECURED TO WALL, CUT D and E TO LENGTH REQUIRED FOR A SNUG FIT.

You will now have two basic sections, Illus. 12. Place two end sections in position. Check with level. Fasten end sections to studs in wall using 2″ No. 12 flathead wood screws or #10 common nails, or toenail to floor.

Cut shelves F to size required and nail into position. Nail F to C E, B D, Illus. 12.

Rails D and E for center section can be cut to length required and toenailed in position with 6 penny finishing nails, Illus. 13.

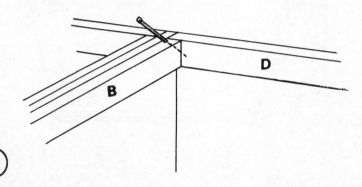

Cut top G, Illus. 14 to length required. Use clear pine, no knots, 1x12 and 1x6. Cut to width required to maintain overall width of 16⅞″. Apply glue and fasten together with ⅜″ corrugated fasteners through bottom side only. Keep wide board in front. Keep two boards clamped together until glue has a chance to set time prescribed by glue manufacturer. Nail G to ends and partitions with 6 penny finishing nails, Illus. 15.

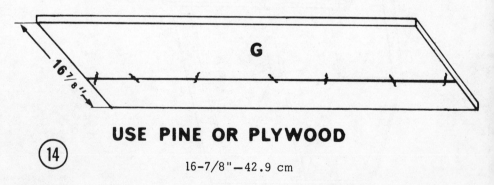

USE PINE OR PLYWOOD

16-7/8″—42.9 cm

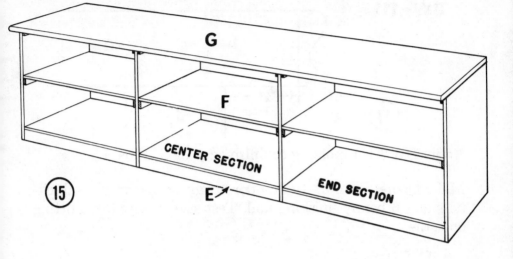

Countersink heads. Fill holes with woodfiller for painting; use matching Putty Stik for hardwood.

Cut 5/4 x 4 to 3″ width, by length required for H, Illus. 16. Nail 5/4 x 3 (2½″ wide) in position shown for J. Cut four stiles K, use 5/4 x 3 by length required. Nail in position shown. Center K over edge of partitions.

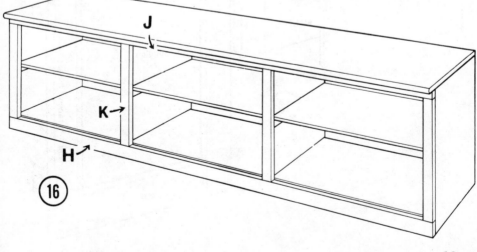

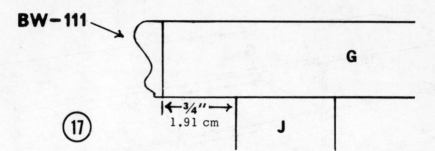

BW-111

G

|← 3/4" →|
1.91 cm

J

(17)

Apply BW #111 molding to finish edge of G, Illus. 17.

Make Doors, Illus. 18. Build door height of opening less thickness of a 6 penny finishing nail. Test size required by cutting one stile.

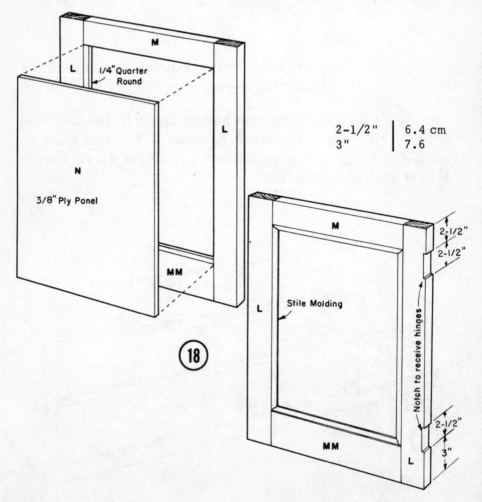

M

L   1/4" Quarter
     Round

L

N

3/8" Ply Panel

MM

| 2-1/2" | 6.4 cm |
| 3" | 7.6 |

M

2-1/2"

2-1/2"

Stile Molding

L

Notch to receive hinges

2-1/2"

3"

MM

L

(18)

Cut stiles L from 5/4 x 3. Rail M from 5/4 x 3; rail MM from 5/4 x 4. Apply glue and fasten together with two ⅜″ corrugated fasteners at each corner, driven across grain in back, Illus. 19.

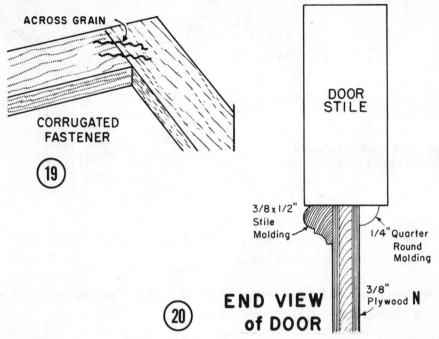

ACROSS GRAIN

CORRUGATED FASTENER

19

DOOR STILE

3/8 x 1/2″ Stile Molding

1/4″ Quarter Round Molding

3/8″ Plywood N

20 END VIEW of DOOR

Countersink fasteners, fill holes with wood filler, sandpaper smooth.

Miter-cut ¼″ quarter round molding to fit around inside edge, Illus. 20. Apply glue and nail in place with ¾″ or 1″ brads in position indicated.

Cut ⅜″ plywood panel N to fit opening, Illus. 18. Apply glue and place N in position. Miter-cut ⅜ x ½ stile or glass bead molding to fit around outside face. Apply glue and nail in place. Countersink brads. Fill holes with wood filler.

Notch L and K to receive 2½″ x 1¹¹⁄₁₆″ loose pin butt hinges, Illus. 18. Locate hinges 2½″ from top, 3″ from bottom. Plane doors to fit.

Bore holes to receive door pull, or knob, 10″ down from top of door, ¹⁵⁄₁₆″ from outside edge, Illus. 21.

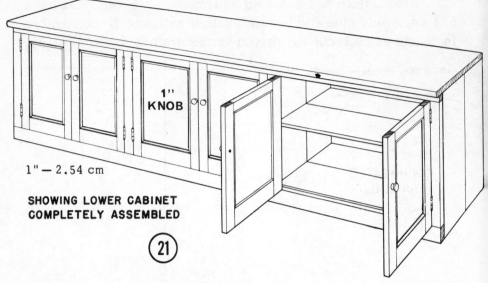

1" KNOB

1" — 2.54 cm

SHOWING LOWER CABINET
COMPLETELY ASSEMBLED

㉑

Fasten bullet type door catch or equal to door and to shelf. Follow manufacturer's directions.

Cut two 1 x 2 to length required for O and P. Nail to wall and P to ceiling in position shown, Illus. 22.

If ceiling joists run parallel to P, use expansion fastener, Illus. 22, to secure P in place.

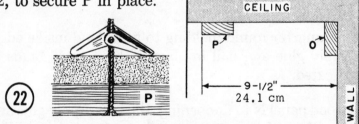

CEILING

P

O

9-1/2"
24.1 cm

WALL

P

㉒

Cut Q, Illus. 23, to length required. Use ¾" plywood or 1 x 10. Notch top edge to receive O and P.

Cut metal shelf standards, Illus. 29, to length required. Screw in position indicated, Illus. 23. Shelf standards have numbered holes to receive brackets. Be sure the same numbered hole in each standard is equal distance from G and in line with each other. Use level. Follow manufacturers directions to install accurately.

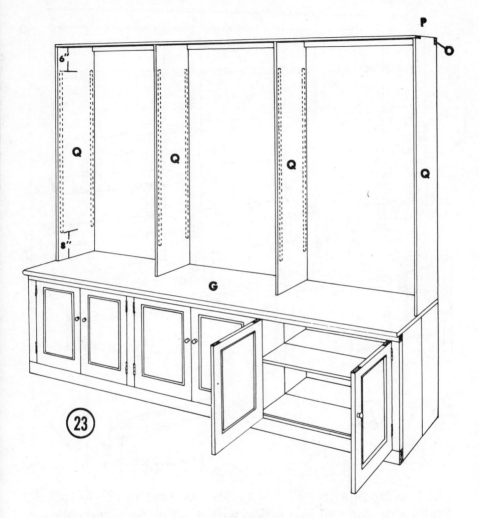

6"

8"

Q

Q

Q

Q

P

O

G

(23)

Apply glue to notches in Q. Position Q over partition in base cabinet. Check both edge and side of each Q with a level. When plumb, toenail Q to P, O and G with 6 penny nails.

Cut 1x6-R, Illus. 24 to length required. Nail in position shown with 6 penny finishing nails.

Cut four stiles S from 1x3. Nail S to Q in position, Illus. 24.

Place shelf brackets in position desired. Cut shelves V to length required from 1x10 or ¾" plywood, Illus. 24.

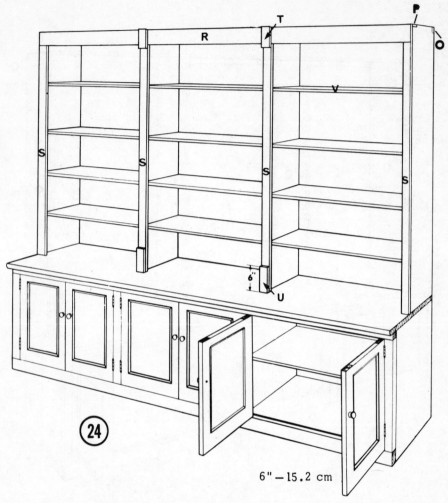

6" — 15.2 cm

Cut two top pilasters T - 5/4 x3x6¼"; two bottom U-5/4 x3x6". Apply glue and nail in position with 4 penny finishing nails.

Cut ¾ x 2¼" pilaster molding to length required and nail in place between U and T, Illus. 24 and 28.

You can finish bookcase at ceiling with ceiling molding to match that on other walls, or use crown molding. If you use ceiling molding follow same procedure suggested for crown molding.

Block crown or ceiling molding in miter box in position shown, Illus. 25. Cut ends of W - 45° to length required to cover R and butt against T.

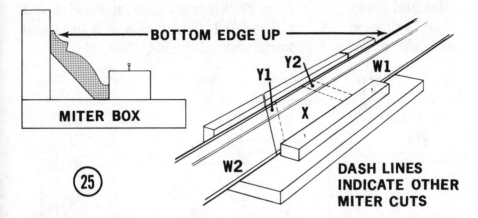

BOTTOM EDGE UP

MITER BOX

Y1 Y2 W1

X

W2

DASH LINES
INDICATE OTHER
MITER CUTS

(25)

Miter cut ends of X and Y to angle shown. When all pieces
are cut to angle and length required they fit together as shown,
Illus. 26, with bottom edge down.

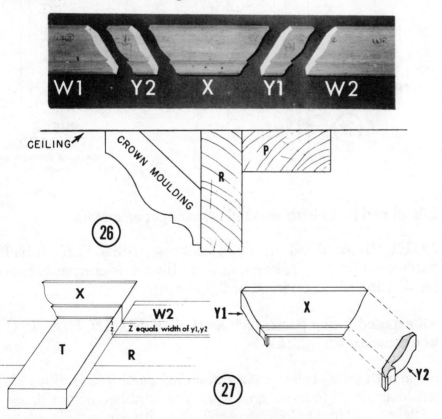

W1 Y2 X Y1 W2

CEILING

CROWN MOULDING

P

R

(26)

X

T

W2

Z equals width of y1,y2

R

Y1

X

Y2

(27)

Bottom edge of X equals width of T, Illus. 28.

Glue and brad X to Y1, Illus. 27. When glue sets, apply glue and brad assembled XY1 to T and W1. Glue and brad X to Y2 and W2. Use a nailset to countersink nailheads, Illus. 28.

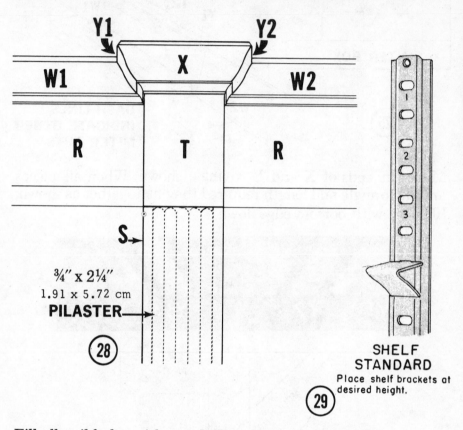

¾" x 2¼"
1.91 x 5.72 cm
PILASTER

(28)

SHELF STANDARD
Place shelf brackets at desired height.

(29)

Fill all nail holes with wood filler, sandpaper smooth.

NOTE: If you decide to build bookcase with ¼" prefinished hardwood plywood, make a sandwich, Illus. 6, as previously outlined, using ½" fir plywood or flakeboard.

All exposed facing parts, such as H, J, K M, MN, R, S, T, U would measure 1" thick.

Since both sides of the two face standing partitions Q, Illus. 23, would also need to be covered with ¼" prefinished plywood, use ½" flakeboard for Q. Cover exposed edge with paper-thin matching wood tape.

FREE STANDING BOOKCASE

A free standing bookcase, Illus. 30, measuring 35½″ wide, 6′6¾″ high, can be built from 1 x 12 clear pine, surfaced four sides (S4S). Cut B, E, H and top shelf to length required.

LIST OF MATERIALS

Use clear, select pine or ¾″ plywood surfaced two sides.
1x2 — 2/8
1x3 — 1/8, 1/12
1x12 — 2/12, 1/14
¼″x36x96 fir plywood good two sides
8 lineal ft. shelf standard shelf standard brackets
4 prs cabinet door hinges
4 magnetic catches
4 — 1″ door knobs or door hardware to suit.

Take a door to your glass retailer, let him cut glass to fit.

Cut two sides A — 1x12x6′ 6¾″, Illus. 31. Using a table saw, electric or hand saw, notch full length of back edge ¼″ deep, ½″ wide, to receive ¼″ plywood back D, Illus. 32, 33.

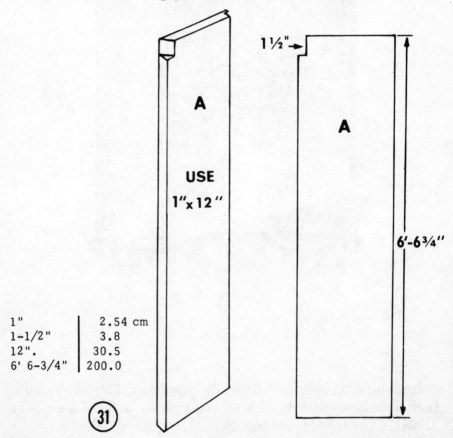

1″	2.54 cm
1-1/2″	3.8
12″.	30.5
6′ 6-3/4″	200.0

A

USE
1″x 12″

1½″→

A

6′-6¾″

③①

Saw top front inside edge to 45°, 1½" down, Illus. 32.

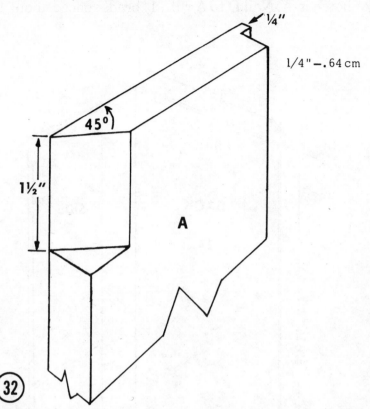

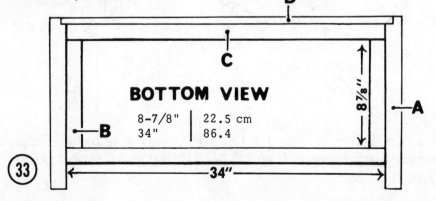

Cut two cleats B, Illus. 33, 1x2x8 ⅞". Cut two cleats C, 1x2x34". Apply glue and nail C to B with two 4 penny finishing nails at each joint.

Apply glue and screw B to A, keeping B and C flush with bottom of A, Illus. 33.

Cut ¼" plywood back D — 35 x 6' 6¾", Illus. 34. Apply glue to ¼" notch in A. Nail D to A with 1" brads spaced about 12" apart.

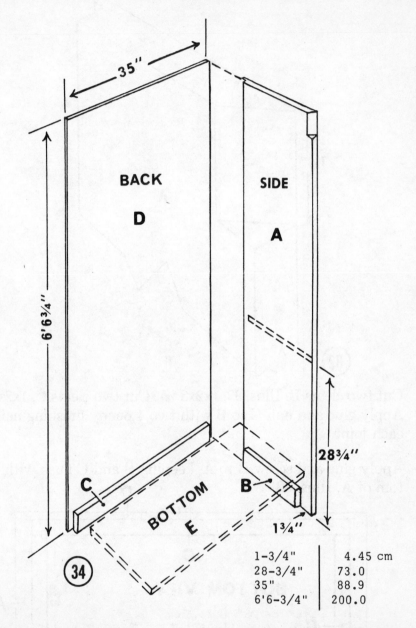

1-3/4"	4.45 cm
28-3/4"	73.0
35"	88.9
6'6-3/4"	200.0

Cut two shelves E from 1 x 12 x 34". Apply glue to back edge and ends, and to top of B and C. Nail E to B and C with 4 penny nails, Illus. 35.

30

Check assembly with square and nail D to E. Nail top shelf E
28¾" from bottom of A, Illus. 34.

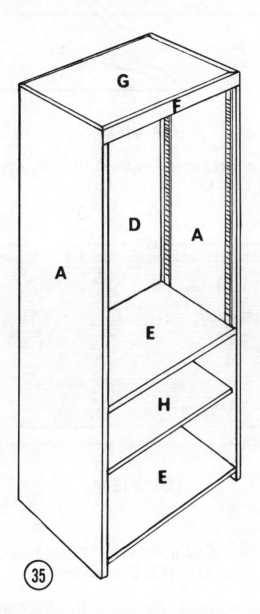

After assembling A, B, C, D and E, check size of all parts before
cutting.

Miter-cut ends of 1x2x35½″, Illus. 36, 37 for F. Glue and nail to A in position shown, Illus. 35.

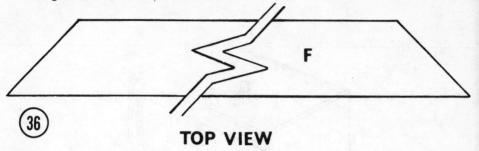

F

(36)

TOP VIEW

Cut top G from 1x12 to size required, Illus. 37. Apply glue and nail A, F and D to G.

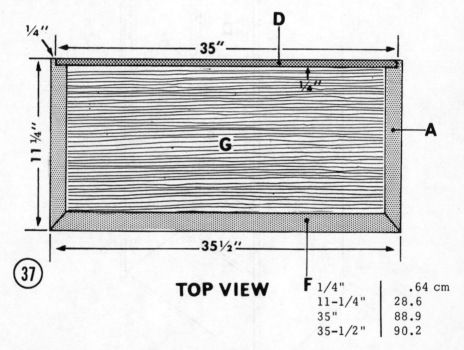

(37)

TOP VIEW

F	1/4"	.64 cm
	11-1/4"	28.6
	35"	88.9
	35-1/2"	90.2

Cut shelf H, Illus. 35, from 1x10⅝x34″ or width required. Apply glue and nail A and D to H in position shown.

Countersink all nailheads, fill holes with wood filler.

Cut metal shelf standards to length required to fit in position shown, Illus. 38 and 39. Notches in standards are numbered. Cut each to match others.

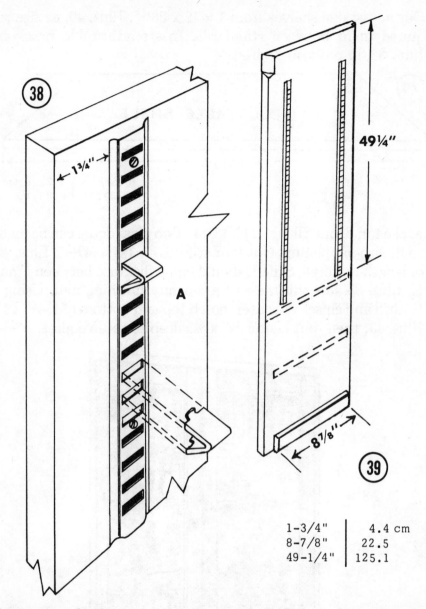

1-3/4"	4.4 cm
8-7/8"	22.5
49-1/4"	125.1

Fasten standard to A, 1¾″ from front; 1″ from D. Fasten front standard in place with one screw at top. Check with level, then fasten other screws. Place rear standard in position, use level to make certain the same numbered notch is in line. After putting in top screw, use level to make certain it's plumb. Use level to draw lines across D, then on A, to level up standards on other side.

Cut adjustable shelves from 1 x 12 x 33½″, Illus. 40, to size required to fit between standards. Insert adjustable brackets, Illus. 38, in position desired.

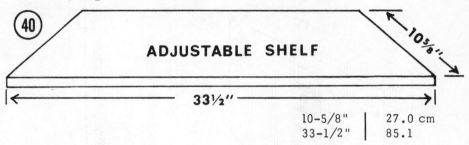

ADJUSTABLE SHELF

33½″

10-5/8″

10-5/8"	27.0 cm
33-1/2"	85.1

Make top doors, Illus. 41, 42, 43, 44. Two glass doors can be made to fit size of opening. Cut four stiles L — 1x1¾x47½″, Illus. 42, or length required. Stile L should equal distance between F and E, Illus. 35, less thickness of a 6 penny finishing nail. Using a ¼″ drill and chisel, or router, notch top and bottom of L-¼″ x 1″, Illus. 43; then rout center ⅛″ x ⅝″ deep to receive glass.

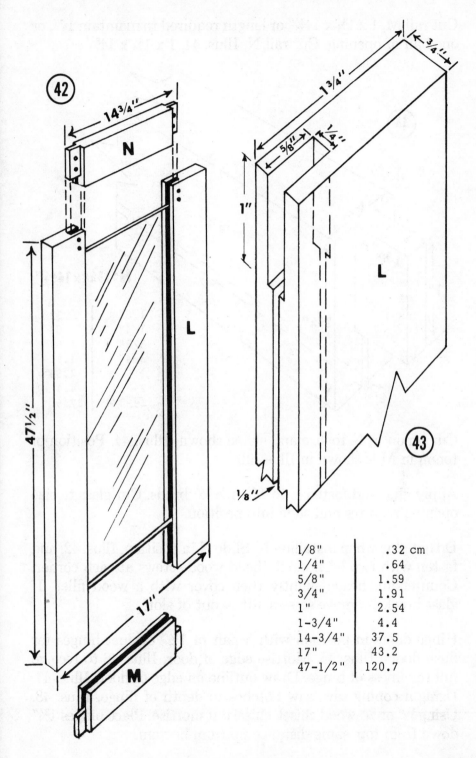

1/8"	.32 cm
1/4"	.64
5/8"	1.59
3/4"	1.91
1"	2.54
1-3/4"	4.4
14-3/4"	37.5
17"	43.2
47-1/2"	120.7

Cut rail M, 1 x 1¾ x 14¾″ or length required to maintain 17″, or one half of opening. Cut rail N, Illus. 44, 1 x 1¾ x 14¾″.

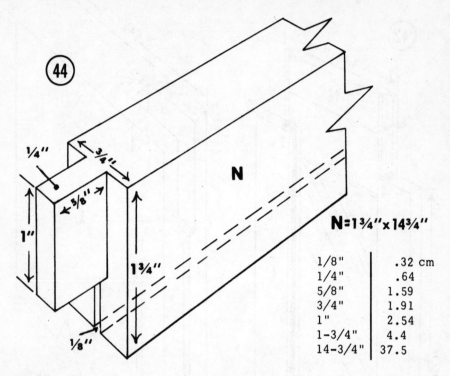

1/8″	.32 cm
1/4″	.64
5/8″	1.59
3/4″	1.91
1″	2.54
1-3/4″	4.4
14-3/4″	37.5

Cut tenon in N to size and shape shown, Illus. 44. Position of tenon in M is shown in Illus. 42.

Apply glue and fasten L to M with ½″ brads. Cut glass to size opening requires and slide into position.

Do not glue when installing N. Slide N in position, Illus. 42, and fasten with two ½″ no. 6 flathead wood screws at each corner. Countersink heads slightly then cover with a wood filler. If glass breaks, remove screws, lift N out of slot.

Hinge doors in position with a pair of 1½″ cabinet hinges for flush doors, Illus. 45. Mortise edge of door, Illus. 46 to receive full thickness of hinge. Draw outline on edge of door, Illus. 47. Using a coping saw, saw notches to depth of hinge, Illus. 48. Using ½″ or ¾″ wood chisel, chisel out mortise. Place hinges 1¾″ down from top, same distance up from bottom.

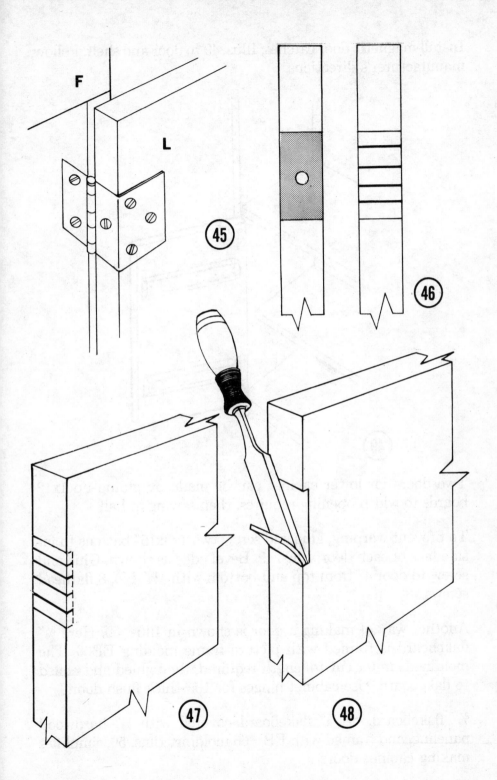

Install magnetic door catches, Illus. 49 to door and shelf. Follow manufacturer's directions.

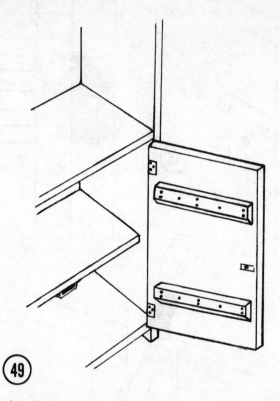

(49)

Two doors for lower cabinet can be made by gluing up 1x12 boards to width opening requires, then sawing in half.

To prevent warping, glue and screw two 1x3x15″ battens to inside face of each door, Illus. 49. Bevel edge as shown. Glue and screw to door 4″ from top and bottom with 1¼″ No. 8 flathead screws.

Another way of making a door is shown in Illus. 50. Here ¾″ flakeboard is framed with picture frame molding EB66. The molding is miter cut to length required, then glued and nailed to flakeboard. Use cabinet hinges for 1⅛″ thick flush doors.

¾″ flakeboard, or ½″ flakeboard covered with ¼″ hardwood paneling, and framed with EB #66 molding, Illus. 50, simplifies making cabinet doors.

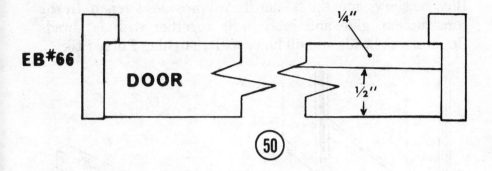

EB#66

DOOR

¼"

½"

(50)

Apply 1″ door knobs. These can be fastened at center, 1″ in from edge.

A free standing, prefinished hardwood plywood bookcase can be made by gluing ¼″ prefinished plywood to both sides of ⅜″ flakeboard. When edge banded with matching wood tape, or equal paper thin veneer, it makes a handsome, professional looking cabinet. Cut parts size required.

Doors can be made with two thicknesses of prefinished plywood plus a core of ⅛″ hardboard, Illus. 51. By cutting the hardboard ⅝″ less than width of stile L and rail M and N, you provide a channel for glass.

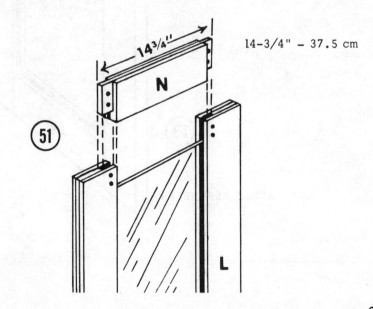

14-3/4" – 37.5 cm

Illus. 52 shows how the ⅛″ hardboard provides a tenon. In this construction, glue and brad parts together with ½″ brads. Countersink heads and fill holes with matching Putty Stik.

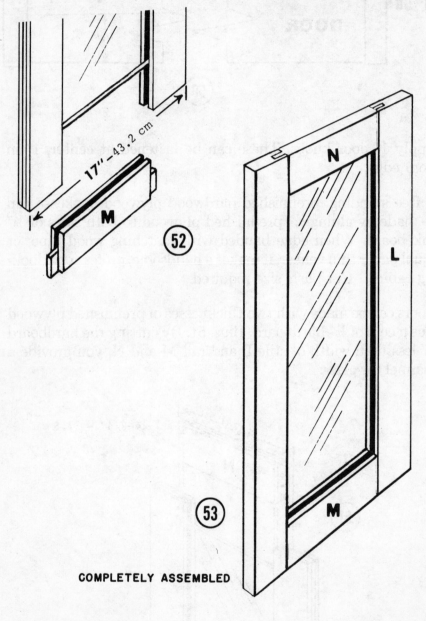

17″—43.2 cm

M

52

N

L

53

M

COMPLETELY ASSEMBLED

SECTIONAL BOOKCASES

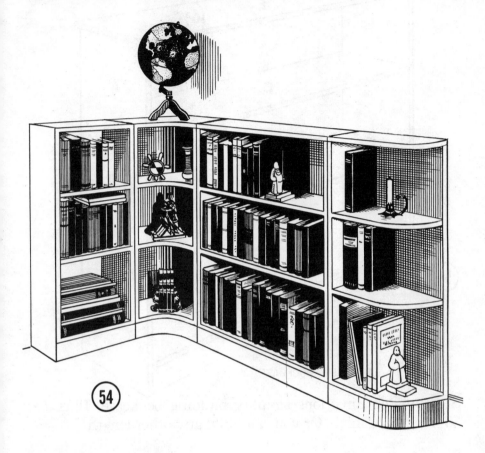

LIST OF MATERIALS

Bookcase Illus. 54

    1 — 1x12x16′
    1 — 1x12x4′
    1 — 1x2x6′
    2 doz. 1½ No. 10 flathead wood screws
    1 lb. 6 penny finishing nails
    Glue

These can be built to fit space available, Illus. 54. Buy clear, or shelving grade pine with tight knots. Parts can be cut from 1x12 and built full width (11¼″) ; or parts can be cut from ¾″ plywood to width indicated, Illus. 55.

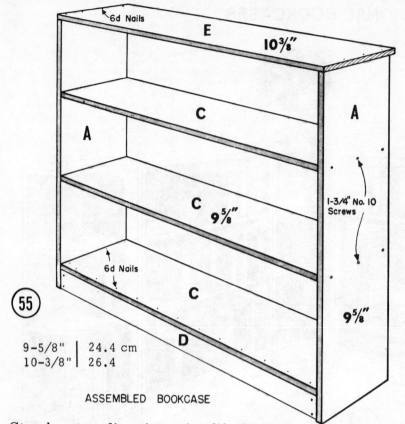

E

10⅜"

C

A

A

6d Nails

1-3/4" No. 10
Screws

C

9⅝"

6d Nails

C

9⅝"

55

D

| 9-5/8" | 24.4 cm |
| 10-3/8" | 26.4 |

ASSEMBLED BOOKCASE

Step-by-step directions simplify building bookcase, Illus. 55, 36" long, 36½" high. Or you can build any other length.

Since 1x12 or ¾" plywood will only support a limited amount of weight, build to 36" length; or install shelf supports, Illus. 56, every 30" to 36" for longer units.

Sides should be screwed to shelves. To make like a "pro," countersink screw heads. Use a pilot hole bit or by drilling a ⅜" hole, ¼" or ⅜" deep, Illus. 57, then a ³⁄₁₆" through A. Cut ⅜" dowel length required. After driving screw, glue dowel in position, sandpaper smooth. Or you can use a screw pilot bit, Illus. 58, to countersink screw head. In this case cover head of screw with wood filler. Always bore shank hole large enough to freely accommodate screw shank. Bore pilot hole slightly less than diameter of threaded portion of screw and only half the depth of threaded portion.

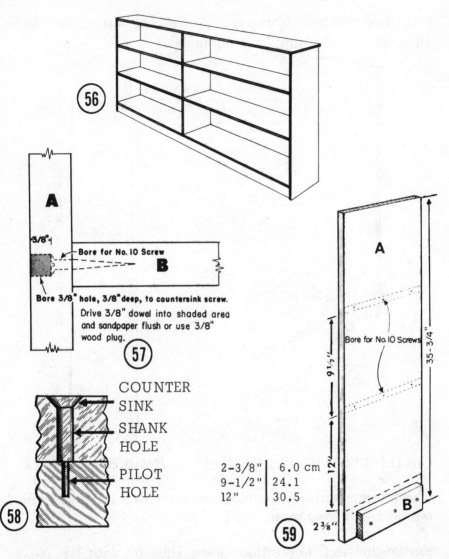

A

3/8"

Bore for No. 10 Screw

B

Bore 3/8" hole, 3/8" deep, to countersink screw.
Drive 3/8" dowel into shaded area
and sandpaper flush or use 3/8"
wood plug.

57

COUNTER
SINK

SHANK
HOLE

PILOT
HOLE

58

2-3/8"	6.0 cm
9-1/2"	24.1
12"	30.5

A

Bore for No. 10 Screws

9 1/2"

35 - 3/4"

12"

B

2 3/8"

59

Cut two A from − 1x12x35 ¾", Illus. 55. Bore three screw holes
for each shelf where indicated, through outside face of A, Illus.
59; continue drilling ³/₁₆" holes through A to receive #10 screw.

Cut two cleats B 1x1 ½ x 8⅞". Apply glue before nailing or fast-
ening with screws.

Using D as a spacer, screw B to A, Illus. 59, ⅛" up from bottom
of A. By keeping B and D ⅛" from bottom, it simplifies planing
edge if slope in floor requires same.

43

Cut three shelves C from 1x12x34 ½". Nail bottom shelf to B, Illus. 60, with 6 penny finishing nails.

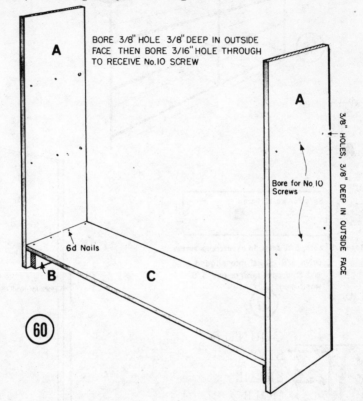

BORE 3/8" HOLE 3/8" DEEP IN OUTSIDE FACE THEN BORE 3/16" HOLE THROUGH TO RECEIVE No.10 SCREW

A

A

3/8" HOLES, 3/8" DEEP IN OUTSIDE FACE

Bore for No. 10 Screws

6d Nails

B   C

(60)

Cut D 1x1 ½x34 ½", Illus. 55. Nail D to B with 6 penny nails.

Check frame with square. Hold square with a 1x2 brace nailed temporarily across front.

Fasten shelves C in position shown, Illus. 59, with 1½" No. 10 screws. Countersink screw heads.

To allow top E, Illus. 55, to butt against wall, cut to width required. Nail in position shown, with E projecting over back edge.

If you want to build a longer one piece bookcase, cut partitions to size required, glue and nail in position.

Toenail middle partitions using 6 penny finishing nails.

44

OPEN END CASE

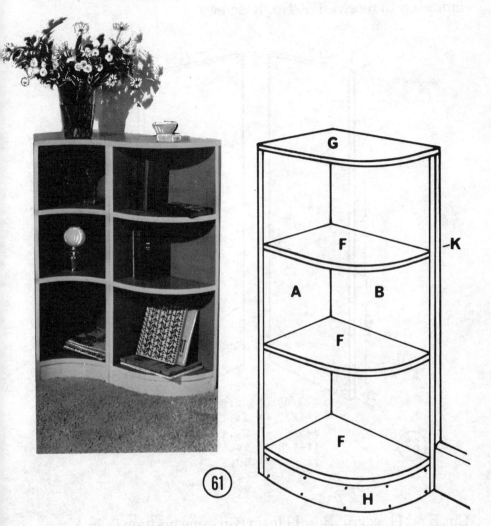

(61)

LIST OF MATERIALS

End Case Illus. 61

    1 — 1x12x12′

    1 — ⅛″ x 1½″ x 2′ hardboard

    2 doz. 1½ No. 10 flathead wood screws

This can be built for right or left end. A right hand bookcase, Illus. 61, can be built in the following way.

Cut one A from 1x12x35 ¾", Illus. 62. Bore six holes in A where indicated to receive 1½" No. 10 screws.

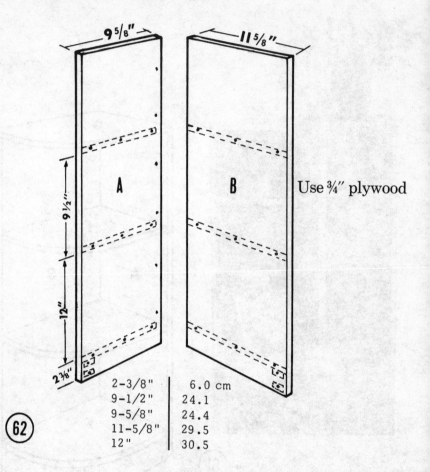

Use ¾" plywood

2-3/8"	6.0 cm
9-1/2"	24.1
9-5/8"	24.4
11-5/8"	29.5
12"	30.5

62

Cut B ¾x11⅝x35¾". Bore holes in B in same position as in A.

Cut cleat C to size and shape shown, Illus. 63, 65, 66. Join pattern with tape and trace outline to size required.

Glue and nail A to B with 6 penny nails. Countersink heads. Nail A and B to C. C is placed ¼" from front edge of A and B, ⅛" up from bottom.

Cut 1x2 filler blocks D, Illus. 64. Nail in position flush with edge of C.

Cut 1x2x1½″ for E, Illus. 64. Screw E in position ⅛″ up from bottom of B.

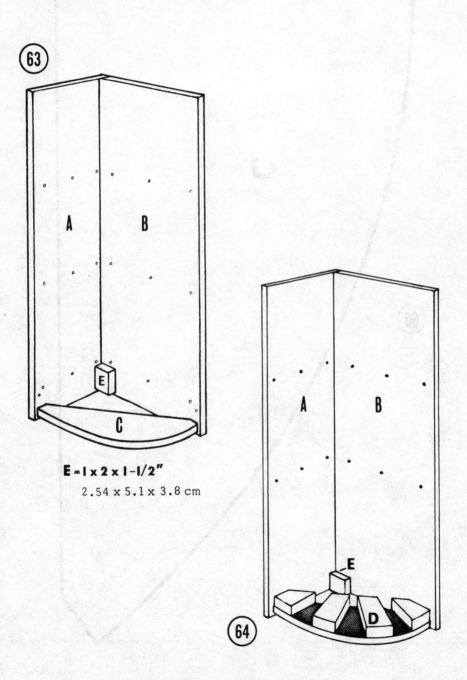

E = 1 x 2 x 1-1/2″

2.54 x 5.1 x 3.8 cm

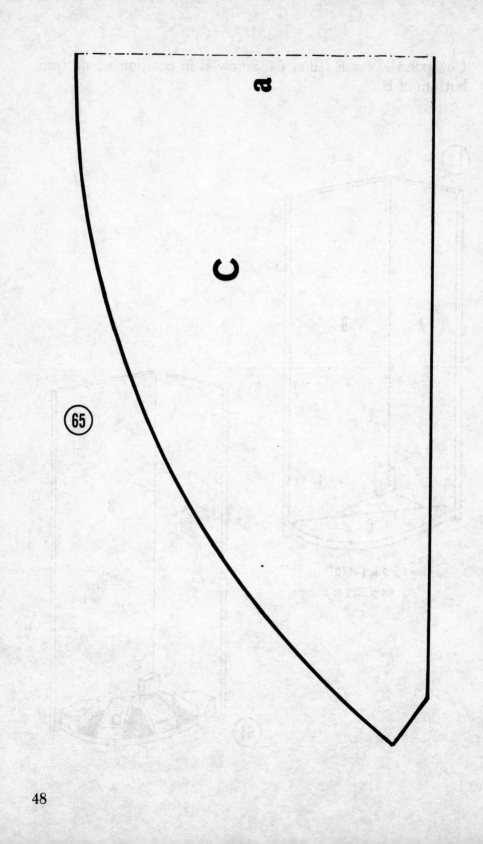

a

C

(65)

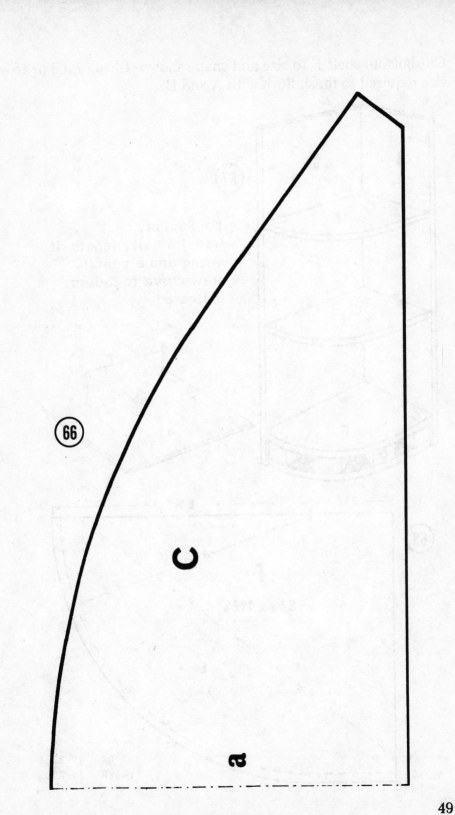

66

C

a

49

Cut bottom shelf F to size and shape shown, Illus. 67, 68 or to size required to finish flush with A and B.

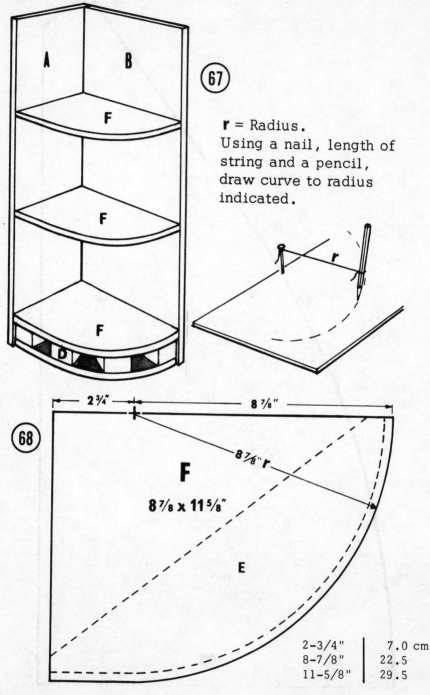

r = Radius.
Using a nail, length of string and a pencil, draw curve to radius indicated.

2-3/4"	7.0 cm
8-7/8"	22.5
11-5/8"	29.5

Nail other shelves in position shown, Illus. 62, or position desired.

Cut top shelf G so it butts against wall. Since a baseboard or baseboard radiation in most rooms will keep a bookcase ¾″ or more away from wall, cut G to size required to butt against wall, Illus. 69.

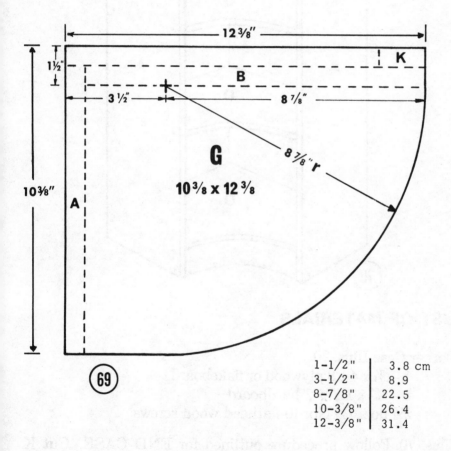

1-1/2"	3.8 cm
3-1/2"	8.9
8-7/8"	22.5
10-3/8"	26.4
12-3/8"	31.4

Cut ⅛″ non-tempered hardboard H ⅛ x 1½″ by length required, Illus. 61. Glue and nail to C and D.

A 1x2 filler K can be cut to length required and nailed to back of B, Illus. 61, 69.

CORNER BOOKCASE

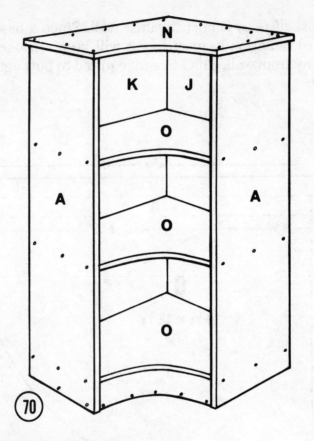

LIST OF MATERIALS

Corner Case Illus. 70
    1 — ¾ x 4 x 8 plywood or flakeboard
    1 — ⅛" x 1½" x 2' hardboard
    2½ doz. 1½ No. 10 flathead wood screws

Illus. 70. Follow procedure outlined for END CASE, Cut K ¾ x 15¾ x 35¾"; J ¾ x 16½ x 35¾", Illus. 71. Cut M from ¾" plywood or pine to size and curve indicated, Illus. 71, 72.

Nail J to K; K and J to M. Nail 1x2x1½ E to J in position shown, Illus. 71. Nail 1x2 D, to M to provide spacers for shelf as shown in Illus. 67.

52

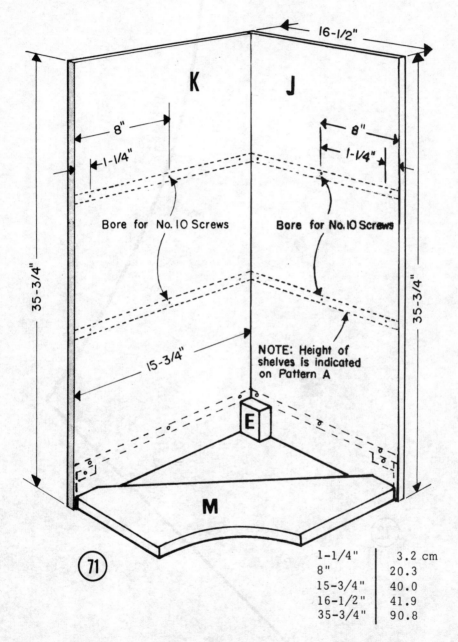

16-1/2"

K   J

8"   8"

1-1/4"   1-1/4"

Bore for No.10 Screws   Bore for No.10 Screws

35-3/4"   35-3/4"

15-3/4"

NOTE: Height of
shelves is indicated
on Pattern A

E

M

71

1-1/4"	3.2 cm
8"	20.3
15-3/4"	40.0
16-1/2"	41.9
35-3/4"	90.8

Cut shelf O to size shown, Illus 73. Cut top N 18″x18″ or size
corner requires, Illus. 74. Finish assembly following procedure
outlined for end bookcase page 45.

Center Line

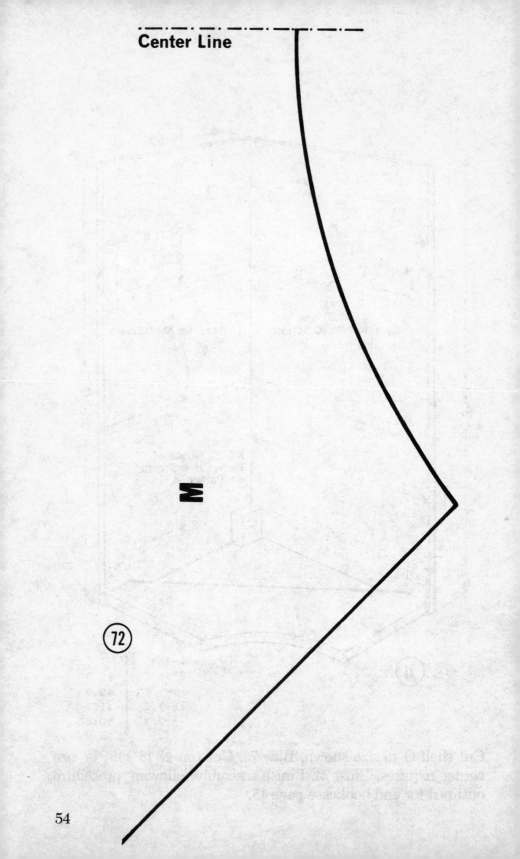

M

(72)

54

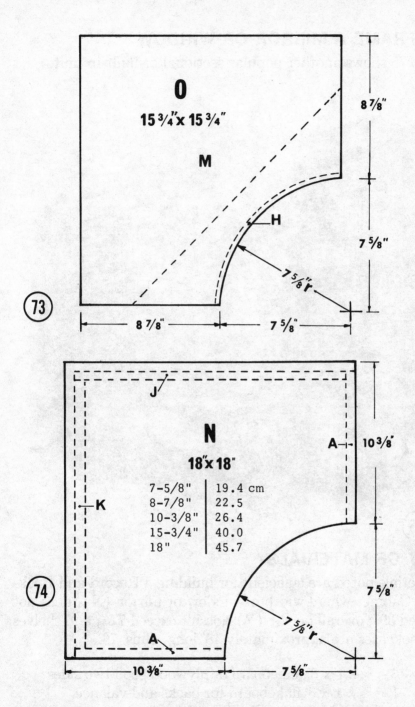

73

O
15 ¾" x 15 ¾"

M

H

8 ⅞"

7 ⅝"

7 ⅝" r

8 ⅞"   7 ⅝"

74

J

N
18" x 18"

7-5/8"	19.4 cm
8-7/8"	22.5
10-3/8"	26.4
15-3/4"	40.0
18"	45.7

K

A

10 ⅜"

7 ⅝"

7 ⅝" r

A

10 ⅜"   7 ⅝"

To compensate for any variation in construction, or variance in thickness of material, always measure a partially assembled unit and cut parts to fit, rather than cut parts to size specified.

TO FRAME A MIRROR OR WINDOW

Illus. 75 shows another popular sectional or built-in unit.

(75)

LIST OF MATERIALS

Materials noted are sufficient for building a Record and Book-case Cabinet where width of window or mirror (X), does not exceed 39″; overall height (Y) doesn't exceed 7′0″; and shelves in bookcases are approximately 18″ long, Illus. 76.

3 — ¾ x 4′ x 8′ flakeboard or plywood good two sides
1 — ⅜ x 4′ x 8′ flakeboard for backs and valance
½ lb. 6d finishing nails
¼ lb. 4d finishing nails
One fluorescent fixture (Optional)

To ascertain size to build bookcases around a window, first measure space needed on each side for draperies. Measure width of window, casing to casing, Illus. 76. Add amount required when drapery is folded. This could be 4″ to 10″ on each side.

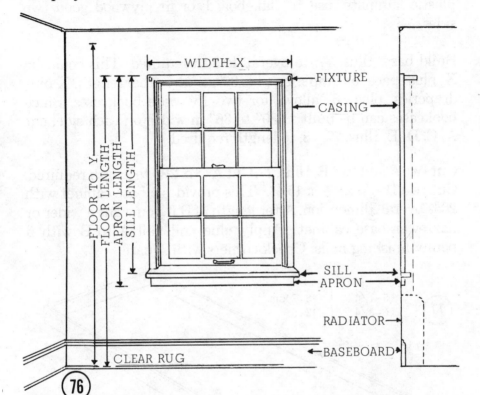

WIDTH-X

FIXTURE

CASING

FLOOR TO Y
FLOOR LENGTH
APRON LENGTH
SILL LENGTH

SILL
APRON

RADIATOR

CLEAR RUG

BASEBOARD

(76)

Next consider length of draperies. Is sill or apron length acceptable? Or do you want them to hang 4″ or 6″ below apron? Build base to acceptable height.

If you want to frame a door with this type of unit on one or both sides, Illus. 30, consider whether you can still move a large chair, table or sofa, in or out of the room, after a bookcase cuts down the area of maneuverability.

If you are building bookcases around a mirror, designers frequently frame the mirror with a wide frame, then build right up to the frame.

Always apply glue before joining parts.

When placing assembled units around a mirror, measure width of X, frame to frame; and from floor to Y.

If you plan on covering base cabinet with a cushion, or with plastic laminate, use ¾″ flakeboard, or fir plywood good two sides.

Build base, Illus. 77, to overall length required. This could be X, plus space for draperies, plus 36″, or any other length. X plus draperies, plus 36″ allows for two 18″ wide bookcases. Since bookcases can be built to 30″ to 36″ in width on each side, cut A, C, D, E, Illus. 77, 78, to length required.

Cut two A and two B, Illus. 77. Cut A – ¾ x 2½″ to length required. Cut two B – ¾ x 2½″ x 15¼″. This provides a base cabinet with 20¾″ overall dimension. Alter length of B if you want a wider or narrower base cabinet. Apply glue and nail A to B with 6 penny finishing nails. Check corners with square.

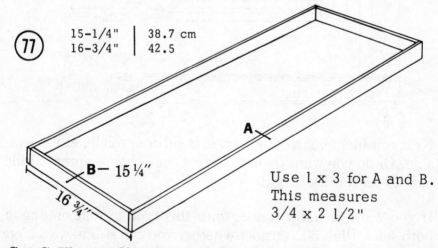

77	15-1/4″	38.7 cm
	16-3/4″	42.5

A

B— 15 ¼″

16 ¾″

Use 1 x 3 for A and B.
This measures
3/4 x 2 1/2″

Cut C, Illus. 78, ¾x19¼″ by length of A. Apply glue and nail C to A and B.

Cut back D, ¾x16″ by length of A, Illus. 78. If you use a 2″ thick cushion, this provides a bench 18¾″ high. Glue and nail D in position to assembled A, B, C.

Cut E – ¾x20¾″ by length of A, Illus. 82.

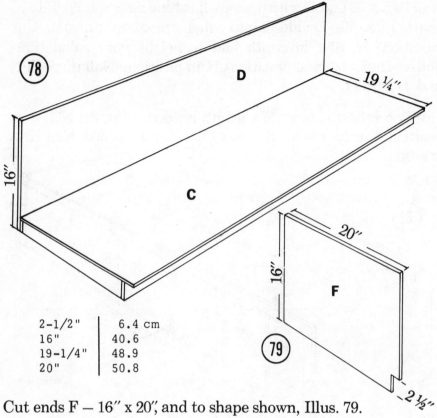

(78)

D

19 ¼"

16"

C

20"

16"

F

(79)

2 ½"

2-1/2"	6.4 cm
16"	40.6
19-1/4"	48.9
20"	50.8

Cut ends F − 16″ x 20″, and to shape shown, Illus. 79.

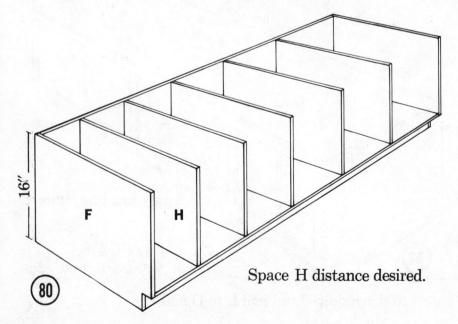

16"

F

H

(80)

Space H distance desired.

Nail F to A, B and D with 6 penny finishing nails spaced 6″ to 8″ apart, Illus. 80. Divide C into equal size compartments. Cut partitions H, 19¼″ in depth and to height your cabinet requires, Illus. 80. Nail partitions H in position. Nail through C and D into H.

Cut two rails J — ¾ x 1½ x length needed, Illus. 81. Nail J in position. Cut four stiles K — ¾ x 1½ x length needed. Nail K in position.

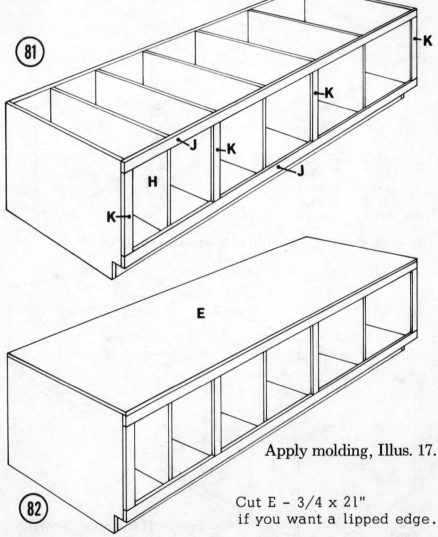

Apply molding, Illus. 17.

Cut E - 3/4 x 21″
if you want a lipped edge.

Cut E to size required and nail E to D and F.

Prior to placing base and bookcases in position, remove shoe molding within area of base. Run BX wiring if you want to install fluorescent lighting. Book No. 694 Electrical Repairs Simplified explains how to install concealed wiring. Fixture can also be connected to an extension cord with a line switch. See page 64.

Place base in position and check with level. If necessary shim base cabinet level with pieces of wood shingle.

Cut bookcase sides L, 9″ by length required, from ¾″ flakeboard, Illus. 83. Notch top ⅜″ x 9″ for valance board.

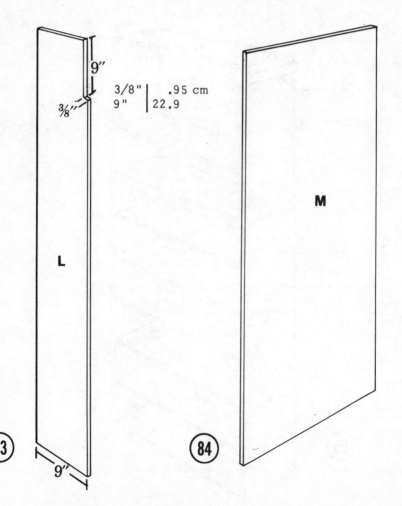

9″

3/8″ | .95 cm
9″ | 22.9

⅜″

M

L

83

84

9″

Cut shelves N to size required. Nail L to N at top and bottom. Square up frame. Cut back M, Illus. 84, to width required, by same length as L. Use ⅜″ plywood for M. Nail back M to L and N. Shelves should be spaced to accommodate your books. Place large books on lower shelves. You can install shelves using shelf brackets as noted on page 32, or nail L to each shelf.

If bookcase is built clear to ceiling, remove ceiling trim within area of bookcase. If you want to fasten BX cable on surface, cut a ceiling panel ¾″ x 8 x length needed. If you conceal BX, cut ceiling panel ¾″ x 8⅝″ by length needed. Cut 1x2 for O, Illus. 85. Screw O in position ¾″ down from top of L.

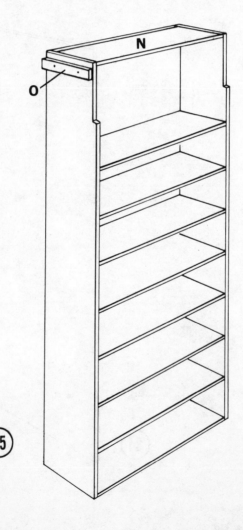

Ceiling panel provides a base for fluorescent fixture and drapery track, Illus. 86. Fasten fluorescent fixture to ceiling panel. Slide ceiling panel in position on top of O, Illus. 85. Fasten ceiling panel to ceiling joists, See Page 22.

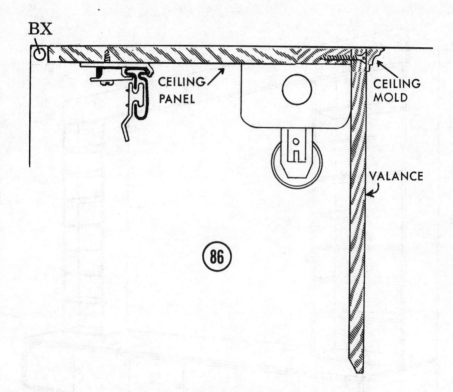

BX

CEILING PANEL

CEILING MOLD

VALANCE

86

Fasten bookcases to wall and/or to base cabinet. Connect BX to lighting fixture.

Cut ⅜ x 9″ x length required for valance, Illus. 86. Nail valance to L and to ceiling panel. Nail ceiling molding to valance.

The front edge of E can be finished with BW-111. See page 20.

Doors can be made to size required following directions on page 20, or from ¾″ flakeboard.

Hinge doors following directions on page 36. Doors should meet over center of H. Fasten roller door catches to both sides of H.

After painting cabinet, or veneering with woodgrain plastic laminate, drill holes and install 1″ brass door pulls, Illus. 87, following directions on page 21.

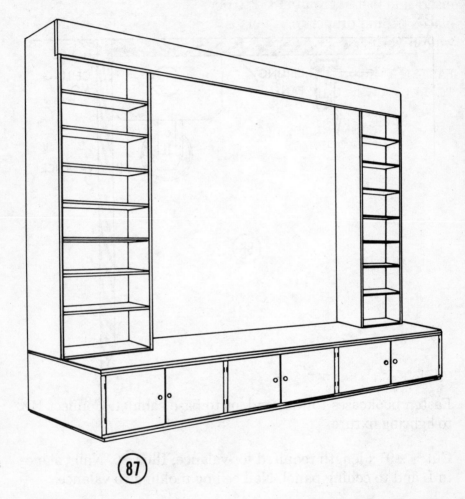

87

WIRING

Fluorescent lighting, as described in this book, performs best when used on a grounded wiring system. It is a simple matter to wire fluorescent channel with a grounding type extension cord to wall outlet.

Illus. 88 shows how this is done with a switch in cord. 3w type "SJ" 18 gauge, heavy duty cord should be used to connect channel to wall outlet. Use polarized rubber plug and adapter. Install switch in line at convenient height. Fasten plug in cord, Illus. 89. Insert adapter in wall outlet. Loosen screw on wall plate, insert and fasten ground lead to plate. Since the cord is usually placed behind draperies, it makes an inexpensive, easy and safe way of wiring.

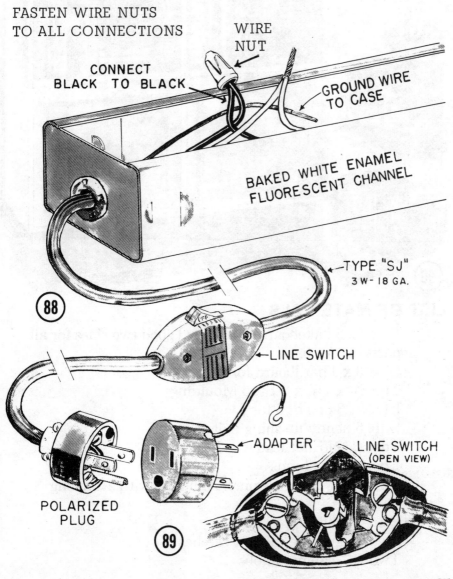

FASTEN WIRE NUTS
TO ALL CONNECTIONS

WIRE NUT

CONNECT BLACK TO BLACK

GROUND WIRE TO CASE

BAKED WHITE ENAMEL FLUORESCENT CHANNEL

TYPE "SJ" 3W-18 GA.

88

LINE SWITCH

POLARIZED PLUG

ADAPTER

LINE SWITCH (OPEN VIEW)

89

BOOKCASE RECORD CABINET

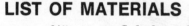

(90)

LIST OF MATERIALS

¾″ x 4 x 8 flakeboard or plywood good two sides for all parts except back

⅛″ — 3 x 4 hardboard for back

1 pc. ⁷⁄₁₆ x 1⅜″ x 5′ Stop Moulding

EB No. 3 or 4 or 8 for L

½ lb. 6 penny finishing nails

1 doz. 1″ No. flathead wood screws

1 box 1″ wire brads

2 pr. 1½″ x 1½″ loose pin butt hinges with attaching screws

Four 10″ lid supports

Two bullet type cabinet catches

Two 2½″ cabinet knobs

Whether you build this cabinet to size specified or to size that fills space available, you will find it's spacious storage ideal for everything from records to linens and blankets. Some are used as bars. All parts for a 42″ cabinet can be cut from a 4 x 8 panel of ¾″ plywood or flakeboard, Illus. 91.

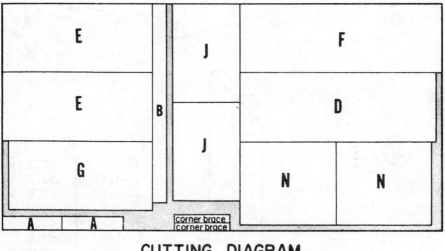

CUTTING DIAGRAM

(91) Showing how to cut parts from a 4 x 8 panel.

Cut two A, Illus. 92, ¾″ x 3″ x 13¼″. Miter ends 45°, Illus. 93, 94.

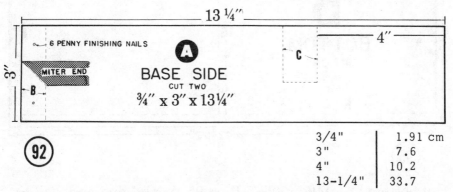

	3/4"	1.91 cm
	3 "	7.6
	4 "	10.2
	13-1/4"	33.7

(92)

Cut one B — ¾″ x 3″ x 42″. Miter ends. Apply glue and nail A B together with 6 penny nails. Check and hold square with temporary brace across top.

Cut two corner braces C, Illus. 93, 1¾″ x 12″. Miter both ends. Keeping A B square, apply glue and nail C to A B.

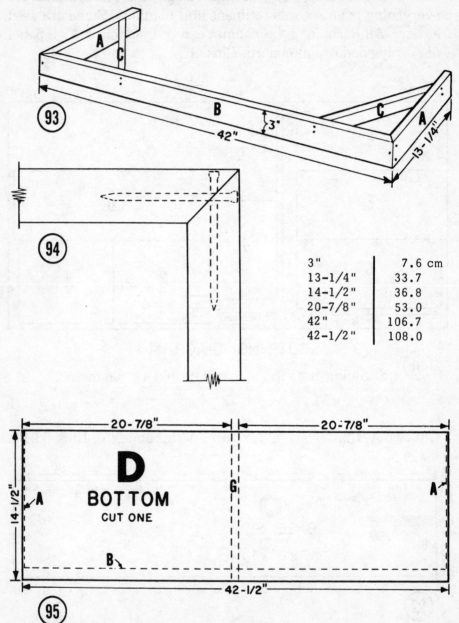

3″	7.6 cm
13-1/4″	33.7
14-1/2″	36.8
20-7/8″	53.0
42″	106.7
42-1/2″	108.0

Cut bottom D — 14½″ x 42½″, Illus. 95, Apply glue and nail D to assembled base with 6 penny nails spaced about 4″ apart, Illus. 96.

68

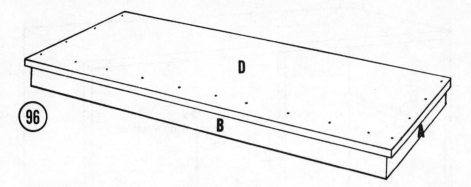

96   D   B   A

Cut two sides E — 14½″ x 33″, Illus. 97. Miter top edge 45° as indicated. Miter cut so E form a pair, one right, one left.

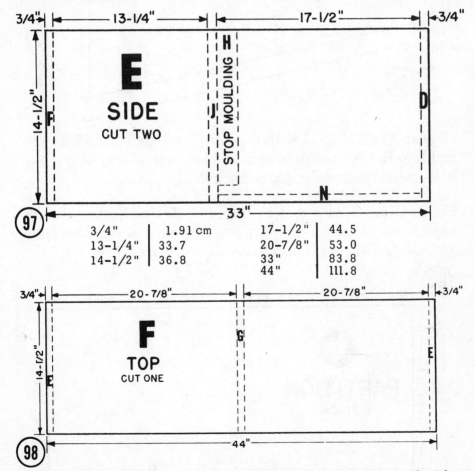

3/4″   13-1/4″   17-1/2″   3/4″

E
SIDE
CUT TWO

14-1/2″   F   H   STOP MOULDING   J   D   N   33″

97

3/4″	1.91 cm	17-1/2″	44.5
13-1/4″	33.7	20-7/8″	53.0
14-1/2″	36.8	33″	83.8
		44″	111.8

3/4″   20-7/8″   20-7/8″   3/4″

F
TOP
CUT ONE

14-1/2″   E   G   E   E   44″

98

Cut top F — 14½″ x 44″, Illus. 98. Miter ends 45° to match sides E, Illus. 99.

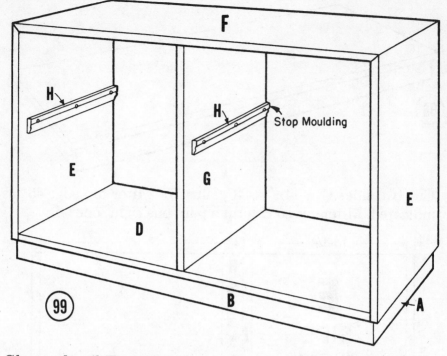

Glue and nail E to D with 6 penny finishing nails. Glue and nail F to E. Check with square. Hold assembly square with 1x2 brace nailed diagonally across back.

Cut partition G, 14½″ x 31½″, Illus. 100. Be sure to check length against assembled unit. Cut to length your unit requires. Glue and nail D and F to G in position shown, Illus. 95, 99.

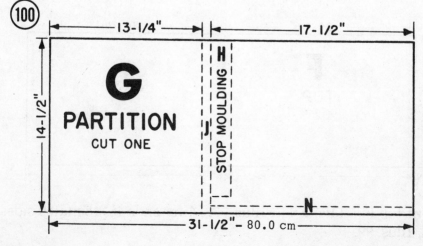

Cut 4 pieces of ⁷⁄₁₆″ x 1⅜″ x 13″ stop molding for shelf support H. Bore through H for No. 8 screws in position indicated, Illus. 99, 100. Glue and screw H in position indicated. Screw H to both sides of G with 1″ No. 8 screws. Stagger position of screws so they don't interfere.

Cut two shelves J — 14½″ x 20⅞″, Illus. 101, or to size your unit requires. Place or nail shelves in position.

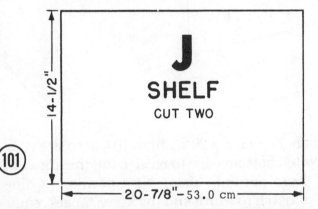

J
SHELF
CUT TWO

14-1/2″

(101)

◄— 20-7/8″ – 53.0 cm —►

Cut back panel K from ⅛″ hardboard. Check assembled cabinet with square before nailing back. Apply glue to D, E, F. Position K about a ¼″ in from outside edge and nail in position with 1″ brads spaced 4″ to 6″ apart.

Miter cut ends of EB carved wood trim or equal ¾″ wide molding L, Glue and brad in position, Illus. 102, 103.

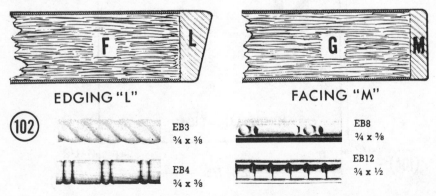

F   L   G   M

EDGING "L"   FACING "M"

(102)

EB3
¾ x ⅜

EB8
¾ x ⅜

EB4
¾ x ⅜

EB12
¾ x ½

For that custom look, use Easi-Bild Carved Wood Trim Nos. 3, 4, 8 or 12 in place of edging L.

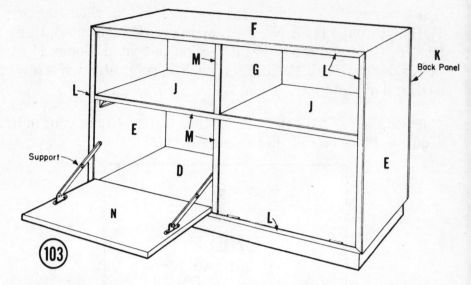

Cut two doors N — 17½″ x 20⅞″, Illus. 104, or to size your cabinet requires. Notch bottom edge to receive full thickness of a closed 1½″ x 1½″ loose pin butt hinge. Note position of hinge, Illus. 103, 104. Cut notch to width and thickness hinges require. Place door in opening. Plane or sandpaper to fit. Hinge N in position using screws retailer recommends.

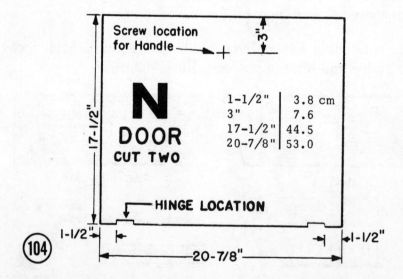

1-1/2″	3.8 cm
3″	7.6
17-1/2″	44.5
20-7/8″	53.0

Prime coat project. When dry, sand smooth, then apply first coat of paint. Sand lightly then apply a second coat.

OPTIONAL TRIM APPLICATION

You can frame a door with BW111 molding as shown in Illus.
105. Miter cut one end, measure and cut a miter 12½". Cut four
pieces 12½". Again miter cut end and cut another miter 15⅞".
Cut four pieces 15⅞". Glue and brad to doors in position indicated.

PROVINCIAL MOLDINGS

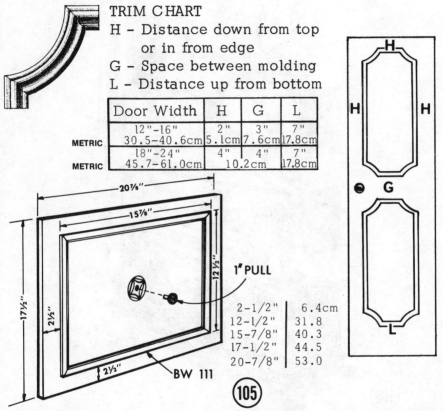

TRIM CHART
H – Distance down from top
    or in from edge
G – Space between molding
L – Distance up from bottom

Door Width	H	G	L
12"–16" 30.5–40.6cm	2" 5.1cm	3" 7.6cm	7" 17.8cm
18"–24" 45.7–61.0cm	4" 10.2cm	4"	7" 17.8cm

METRIC (first row), METRIC (second row)

20⅞"
15⅞"
17½"
2½"
12½"
1" PULL
2½"
BW 111

2-1/2"	6.4cm
12-1/2"	31.8
15-7/8"	40.3
17-1/2"	44.5
20-7/8"	53.0

(105)

Locate center of door by drawing diagonal lines. Drill a hole
through center to receive the door knob. Drill a hole through
center of a BW Rosette to receive bolt in knob. Apply glue to
rosette and fasten door knob in position.

Apply lid supports as shown in Illus. 103. Fasten plunger type
cabinet door catch to center of N and bottom of J, exact distance apart catch requires.

NOTE: Position of shelf permits storing 12" albums.

ROOM DIVIDER

(106)

An easy-to-build room divider, Illus. 106, can be built to any length required. While up to four foot long dividers can be built from clear 1x10 pine, longer units should be built from ¾ x 10. 1x10 will measure 9¼″. This is a good shelf width.

Illus. 107 shows a 40″ and 80″ divider. Construction of both follow the same general procedure. The only difference is the need for shelf supports C in the 80″ unit.

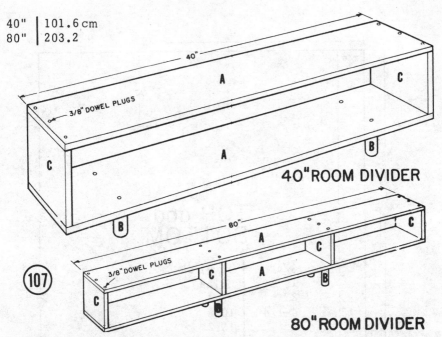

40" | 101.6 cm
80" | 203.2

3/8" DOWEL PLUGS

A

C

A

C

B

40"ROOM DIVIDER

80"

(107)

3/8" DOWEL PLUGS

A

C

C

A

C

B

C

80"ROOM DIVIDER

For a 40″ unit, cut A − 40″. Bore ⅜″ holes ⅜″ deep at ends where indicated, Illus. 108; then bore ³⁄₁₆″ through to receive shank of no. 10 screw. If you use 1″ lumber, a 1¼″ no. 10 screw is sufficient. If you use ⅝″ lumber, use 1½″ no. 10 screw. Note Illus. 109.

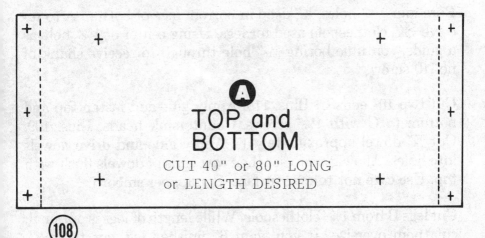

A
TOP and BOTTOM
CUT 40" or 80" LONG
or LENGTH DESIRED

(108)

Bore four ⅜″ holes, ⅛″ deep in top face of bottom A where required for legs B.

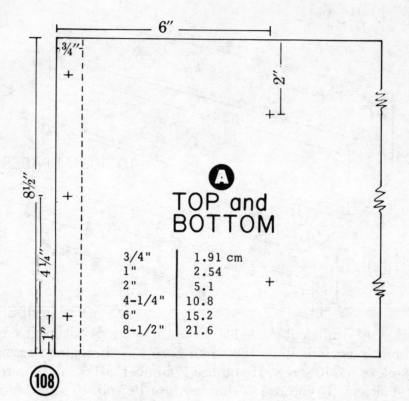

TOP and BOTTOM

3/4"	1.91 cm
1"	2.54
2"	5.1
4-1/4"	10.8
6"	15.2
8-1/2"	21.6

Bore four 1⅜" holes, ¼" deep in bottom face of bottom A to receive 1⅜" clothespole used for legs. Using center of 1⅜" hole as a guide, continue boring ³⁄₁₆" hole through to receive shank of no. 10 screw.

Cut two 10" ends C, Illus. 110. Apply glue and fasten top and bottom to C with 1¼" screws. Countersink heads, Illus. 109. Cut ⅜" dowel approximately 1". Apply glue and drive dowels into holes. Allow glue to set then saw ends of dowels flush with top. Use care not to mar surface. Sandpaper smooth.

Cut legs B from 1⅜" clothespole. While length of legs is optional, cut them oversize. If you want 6" finished leg, cut them 7". Apply glue and insert leg into hole. Secure A to leg with a 2" no. 10 screw, Illus. 109. Fill hole over screw with wood filler or dowel.

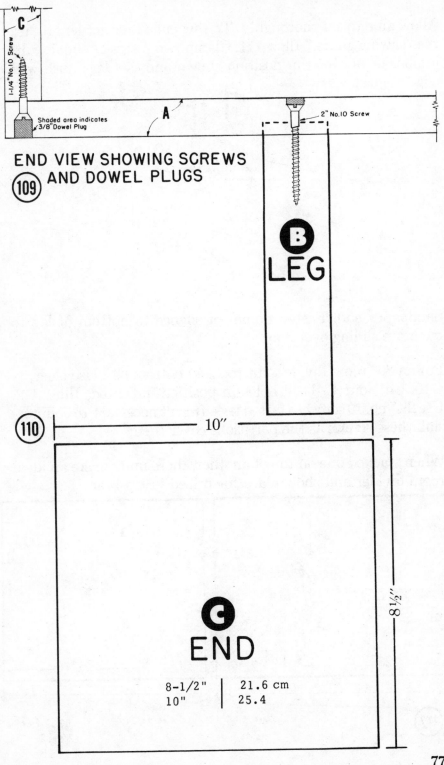

1-1/4" No.10 Screw

C

Shaded area indicates
3/8" Dowel Plug

A

2" No.10 Screw

END VIEW SHOWING SCREWS
(109) AND DOWEL PLUGS

B
LEG

(110) ⟵————— 10″ —————⟶

C
END

| 8-1/2" | 21.6 cm |
| 10" | 25.4 |

8½″

Allow glue to set thoroughly. To saw ends to exact length, use the "sawing guide," Illus. 111. Clamp two pieces of equal width lumber or plywood in position shown and saw legs flush with edge of guide.

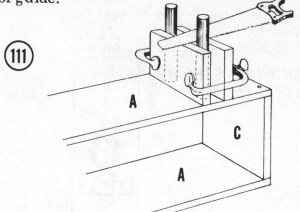

(111)

A

C

A

Sandpaper end. Fasten domes of silence to bottom of leg to facilitate sliding over floor.

For an 80″ room divider, cut top and bottom 80″. Use clear, ⁵⁄₄ x 10. Cut four C. Drill holes in position indicated, Illus. 112. Use 2½″ no. 10 screw to fasten legs. It isn't necessary to countersink these screws as the partitions cover them.

When stacked one on top of another, these units make an ideal room divider and show place for prized bric-a-brac.

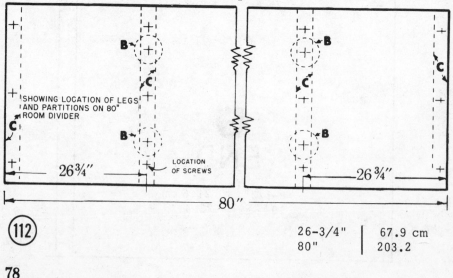

SHOWING LOCATION OF LEGS AND PARTITIONS ON 80" ROOM DIVIDER

B

C

B

C

26¾″

LOCATION OF SCREWS

B

C

B

26¾″

80″

(112)

| 26-3/4" | 67.9 cm |
| 80" | 203.2 |

WALL TO WALL BOOKCASE WITH DRAWERS

A wall-to-wall bookcase with drawers, Illus. 113, can be built to full width of a room; on one or both sides of a door, Illus. 114; or as a free standing unit, Illus. 115, 116. It can be constructed any height and depth desired.

Many lumber and home improvement centers sell preformed plastic drawers. If same are available, space and position drawer guides, Illus. 124, to accommodate same. Directions also explain how to build plywood drawers to fit space allotted.

LIST OF MATERIALS

1x2 for G, R, S and braces
1x3 for A, B and F
1x6 or ¾″ x 5⅝″ x .... for U
1x10 or ¾″ x 9½″ x .... for T and V
¾″ x 4′ x 8′ for C, D, E, H, K, M, N and P
Use ¾″ hardwood, plywood or flakeboard for
C, D, E, H, K, M, N, P, T, U and V.
Pair concealed hinges
Drawer knobs
Carved wood Trim
1¼″ #8 flathead wood screws

⅝″ #5 flathead wood screws
1½″ #7 flathead wood screws
6 penny finishing nails

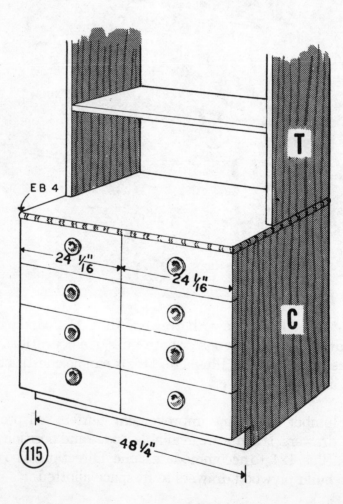

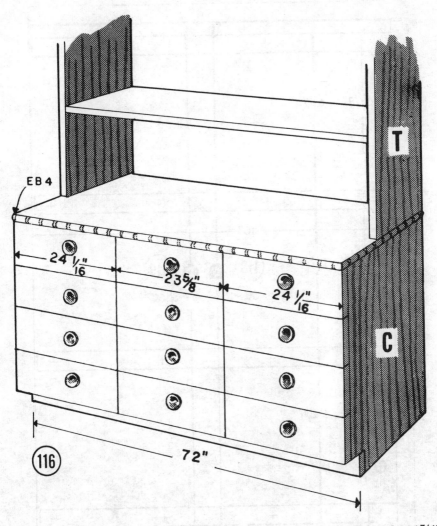

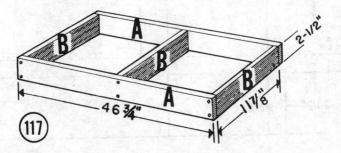

Cut two A from 1x3 to 46¾″, Illus. 117. Cut three B, 1x3x11⅞″. 1x3 will normally measure ¾ x 2½″. Glue and nail A to B with 6 penny finishing nails.

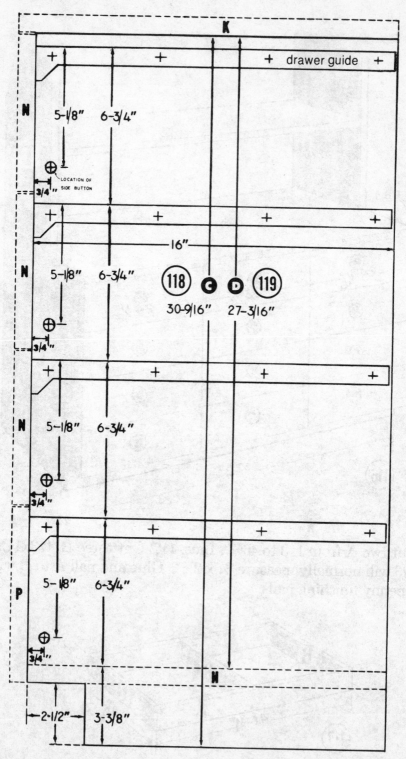

82

Cut C to size noted, Illus. 118, from ¾" plywood. Notch corner 2½" x 2½" or to width of 1x3.

Cut one D to size shown, Illus. 119. Using a square, draw lines on C and D to indicate top edge of drawer guides provided by manufacturer of drawers.

If you prefer to build drawers, use 1x1 aluminum angle, Illus. 120, 121, for drawer guides. A single drawer, Illus. 122, can be built 17" wide; a double drawer 23". Dimensions shown, Illus. 123, allow ⅛" clearance.

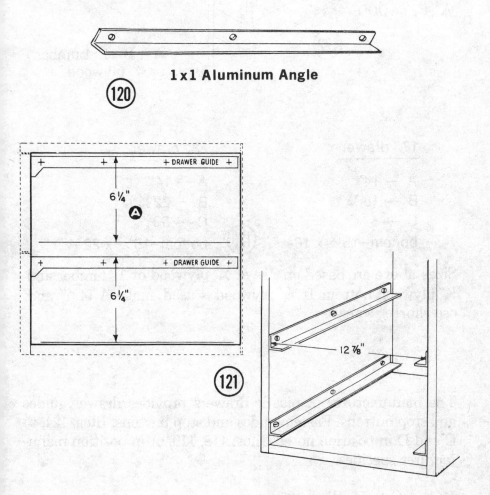

1x1 Aluminum Angle

⑫⓪

+ DRAWER GUIDE +

6 ¼"

Ⓐ

+ DRAWER GUIDE +

6 ¼"

12 ⅞"

⑫①

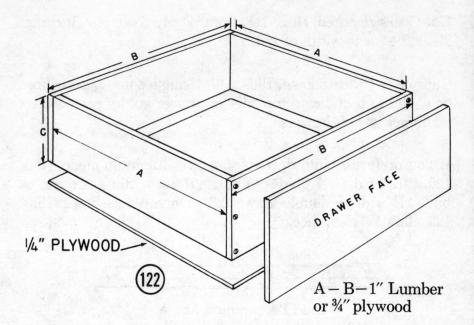

¼" PLYWOOD

(122)

DRAWER FACE

A – B – 1″ Lumber
or ¾″ plywood

17" drawer	23" drawer
A — 14"	A — 14"
B — 16¾"	B — 22¾"
C — 5¾"	C — 5¾"
bottom –15½ x 16¾"	bottom –15½ x 22¾"

(123)

Sizes above are based on use of ¾″ plywood or 1″ lumber and ¼″ plywood bottom. If ⅜″ plywood is used, make A 14¾″ and use shorter screws.

The manufacturer of plastic drawers provides drawer guides and stop buttons. Fasten guides and stop buttons, Illus. 124, to C and D in position noted, Illus. 118, 119, or in position manufacturer specifies.

Fasten C to B, Illus. 125.

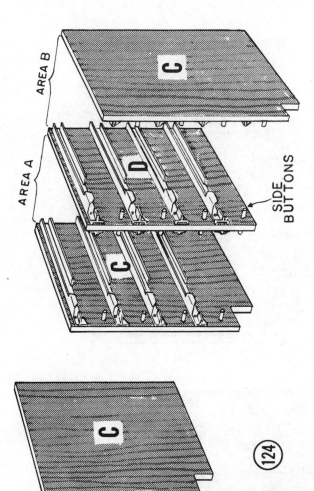

AREA B

AREA A

C

D

SIDE BUTTONS

C

C

(124)

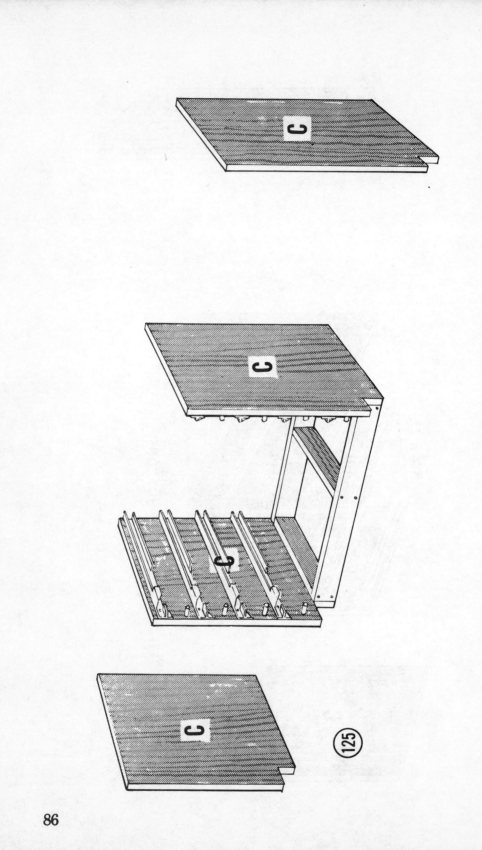

Cut bottom E, Illus. 126, 16 x 46¾″ from ¾″ plywood. Using a square, draw lines 23″ from end. Nail 1x2 braces temporarily along line.

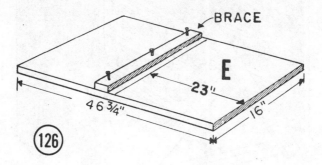

BRACE

E

23″

46¾″

16″

(126)

Apply glue and nail E to D, Illus. 127. Check with level and brace same as shown. Allow glue to set before moving ED.

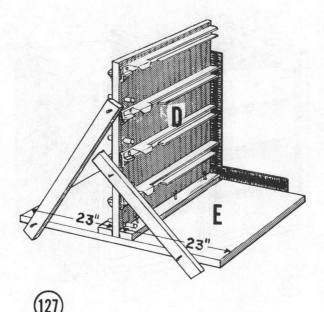

D

E

23″

23″

(127)

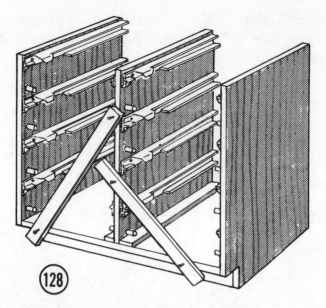

(128)

Fasten E to A, Illus. 128. Remove braces and test plastic drawers in guides. When drawers work smoothly, nail 1x2 braces diagonally across top, Illus. 129.

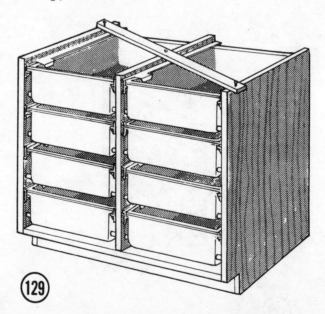

(129)

In a wall-to-wall installation, this unit should be centered as shown, Illus. 130. Cut F to length required. Glue and nail F to B, end C to B. Glue and screw 1x2 shelf support in position shown.

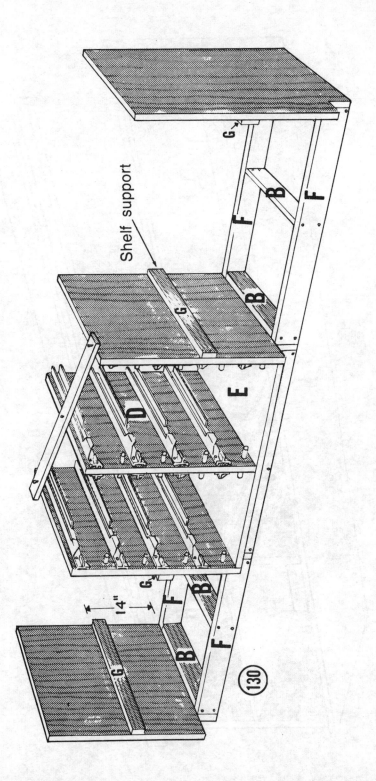

Shelf support

14"

G

F

B

F

B

F

D

E

B

G

G

F

B

F

130

89

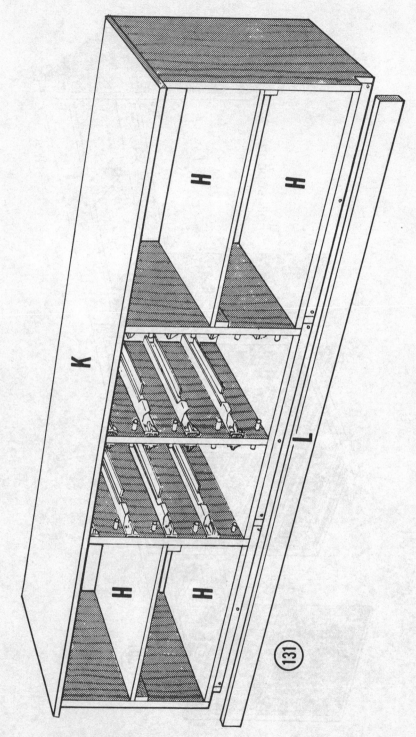

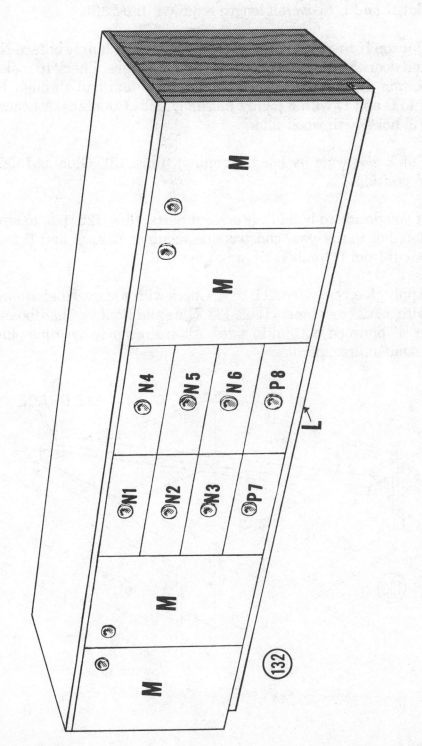

Cut K and L to overall length required, Illus. 131.

Cut top K to width required to finish flush with drawer face N, and doors M, Illus. 118, 132. Remove top brace. Check to make certain drawers move freely. Apply glue and nail through K into C and D with 6 penny finishing nails. Countersink heads. Fill holes with wood filler.

Cut L 2½″ wide by length required, Illus. 131. Glue and nail in position.

If you decide to build drawers, cut parts, Illus. 122, 123, to size noted or to size your construction requires. Sides A and B can be cut from 1″ lumber, ⅝″ or ¾″ plywood.

Apply glue, screw or nail B to A. Check with square. Hold square with a 1x2 cross brace, Illus. 133. Glue and brad ³⁄₁₆″ hardboard or ¼″ plywood bottom to sides. Allow drawer to set time glue manufacturer specifies.

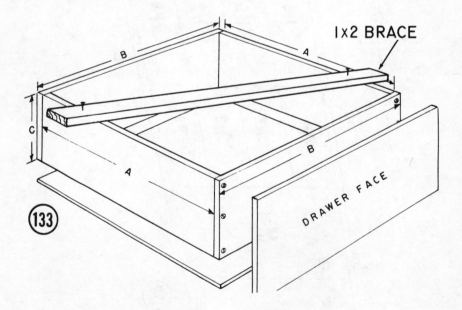

The drawer face can be ½″ plywood plus ¼″ hardwood plywood; 1″ lumber or ¾″ plywood. Build drawers after unit has been assembled. If you want to face drawers and doors with ¼″ prefinished hardwood plywood, cut all drawer faces from one panel so grain runs vertically, Illus. 134. Bottom of drawer fronts P7 and P8 cover edge of E, Illus. 115.

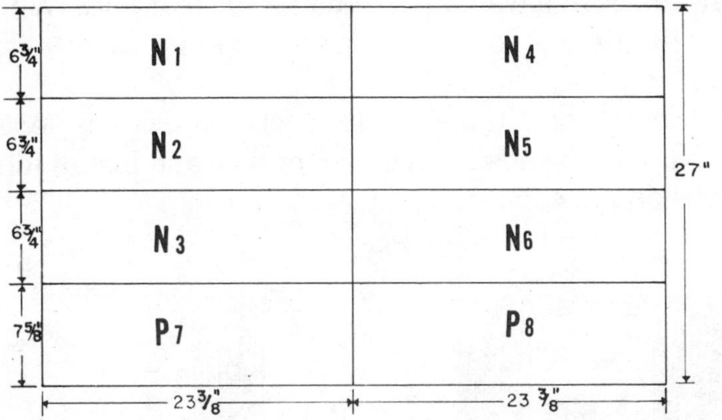

6¾″	N1	N4
6¾″	N2	N5
6¾″	N3	N6
7⅝″	P7	P8

27″

23⅜″ 23⅜″

(134)

Apply glue and fasten B to drawer face. Apply clamp or weight until glue sets. Drill hole at center and fasten one knob in a 17″ drawer, two knobs in a 23″ drawer.

Door M, Illus. 132, should be cut 27⅞″ high by width required. Cut panel to overall size of opening, then cut in half. Plane door to fit opening.

Hinge door to C with a pair of concealed hinges, Illus. 135. Follow hinge manufacturer's directions.

(135)

Cut two 1x2, PO, Illus. 22, to length required. Nail to ceiling following directions on page 22. Note direction of finished flooring on room directly above. Finished flooring is usually nailed across floor joists. Joists are usually spaced 16″ on centers. If joists run parallel to P, drill holes and fasten P to ceiling with expansion fastener, Illus. 22. If joists run at right angles to P, measure 16″ from a wall and try nailing P to a joist. When you drive a nail into one joist, measure 16″ and locate others.

Cut and install partitions Q, Illus. 23, 136, 9½″ by length required. Notch top ends to receive P and O, and install following directions on page 23.

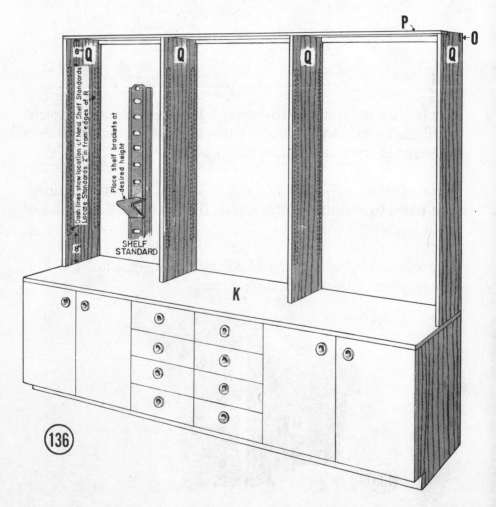

Fasten shelf standards, Illus. 136, to Q in position shown.

Cut twelve shelves V, Illus. 137, 9½″ by length required. Shelves can be cut full length and notched to fit around standards. This locks shelf in position. Insert brackets in standards and cut each shelf to exact size required.

Cut fascia U 5½″ by length required. Glue and nail in position, Illus. 137.

To add a decorator touch, glue and brad carved wood trim in position shown to top of V and to edge of K. On a free standing unit, miter cut front end and apply molding to sides.

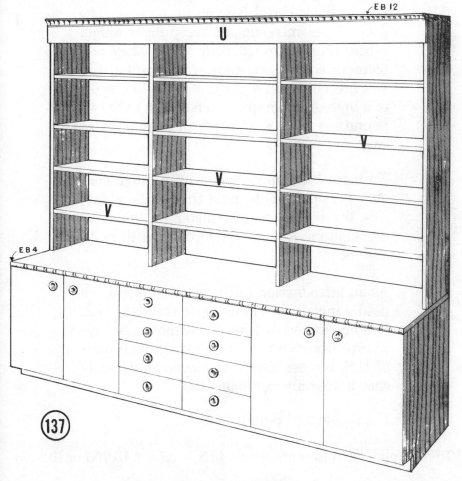

HOW TO THINK METRIC

Government officials concerned with the adoption of the metric system are quick to warn anyone from attempting to make precise conversions. One quickly accepts this advice when they begin to convert yards to meters or vice versa. Place a metric ruler alongside a foot ruler and you get the message fast.

Since a meter equals 1.09361 yards, or 39⅜"+, the decimals can drive you up a creek. The government men suggest accepting a rough, rather than an exact equivalent. They recommend considering a meter in the same way you presently use a yard. A kilometer as 0.6 of a mile. A kilogram or kilo as just over two pounds. A liter, a quart, with a small extra swig.

To more fully appreciate why a rough conversion is preferable, note the 6" rule alongside the metric rule. A meter contains 100 centimeters. A centimeter contains 10 millimeters.

As an introduction to the metric system, we used a metric rule to measure standard U.S. building materials. Since a 1x2 measures anywheres from ¾ to ²⁵⁄₃₂ x 1½", which is typical of U.S. lumber sizes, the metric equivalents shown are only approximate.

Consider 1" equal to 2.54 centimeters;
10" = 25.4 cm.
To multiply 4¼" into centimeters: 4.25 × 2.54 = 10.795 or 10.8 cm.

EASY-TO-USE-METRIC SCALE

DECIMAL EQUIVALENTS

1/32		.03125
	1/16	.0625
3/32		.09375
	1/8	.125
5/32		.15625
	3/16	.1875
7/32		.21875
	1/4	.250
9/32		.28125
	5/16	.3125
11/32		.34375
	3/8	.375
13/32		.40625
	7/16	.4375
15/32		.46875
	1/2	.500
17/32		.53125
	9/16	.5625
19/32		.59375
	5/8	.625
21/32		.65625
	11/16	.6875
23/32		.71875
	3/4	.750
25/32		.78125
	13/16	.8125
27/32		.84375
	7/8	.875
29/32		.90625
	15/16	.9375
31/32		.96875

FRACTIONS — CENTIMETERS

1/16		0.16
	1/8	0.32
3/16		0.48
	1/4	0.64
5/16		0.79
	3/8	0.95
7/16		1.11
	1/2	1.27
9/16		1.43
	5/8	1.59
11/16		1.75
	3/4	1.91

13/16		2.06
	7/8	2.22
15/16		2.38

INCHES — CENTIMETERS

1			2.54
	1/8		2.9
		1/4	3.2
	3/8		3.5
		1/2	3.8
	5/8		4.1
		3/4	4.4
	7/8		4.8
2			5.1
	1/8		5.4
		1/4	5.7
	3/8		6.0
		1/2	6.4
	5/8		6.7
		3/4	7.0
	7/8		7.3
3			7.6
	1/8		7.9
		1/4	8.3
	3/8		8.6
		1/2	8.9
	5/8		9.2
		3/4	9.5
	7/8		9.8
4			10.2
	1/8		10.5
		1/4	10.8
	3/8		11.1
		1/2	11.4
	5/8		11.7
		3/4	12.1
	7/8		12.4
5			12.7
	1/8		13.0
		1/4	13.3
	3/8		13.7
		1/2	14.0
	5/8		14.3
		3/4	14.6
	7/8		14.9

			cm
6			15.2
	1/8		15.6
		1/4	15.9
	3/8		16.2
		1/2	16.5
	5/8		16.8
		3/4	17.1
	7/8		17.5
7			17.8
	1/8		18.1
		1/4	18.4
	3/8		18.7
		1/2	19.1
	5/8		19.4
		3/4	19.7
	7/8		20.0
8			20.3
	1/8		20.6
		1/4	21.0
	3/8		21.3
		1/2	21.6
	5/8		21.9
		3/4	22.2
	7/8		22.5
9			22.9
	1/8		23.2
		1/4	23.5
	3/8		23.8
		1/2	24.1
	5/8		24.4
		3/4	24.8
	7/8		25.1
10			25.4
	1/8		25.7
		1/4	26.0
	3/8		26.4
		1/2	26.7
	5/8		27.0
		3/4	27.3
	7/8		27.6
11			27.9
	1/8		28.3
		1/4	28.6
	3/8		28.9
		1/2	29.2
	5/8		29.5
		3/4	29.8
	7/8		30.2

			cm
12			30.5
	1/8		30.8
		1/4	31.1
	3/8		31.4
		1/2	31.8
	5/8		32.1
		3/4	32.4
	7/8		32.7
14			35.6
16			40.6
20			50.8
30			76.2
40			101.6
50			127.0
60			152.4
70			177.8
80			203.2
90			228.6
100			254.0

FEET —	INCHES —	CENTIMETERS
1	12	30.5
2	24	61.0
3	36	91.4
4	48	121.9
5	60	152.4
6	72	182.9
7	84	213.4
8	96	243.8
9	108	274.3
10	120	304.8
11	132	335.3
12	144	365.8
13	156	396.2
14	168	426.7
15	180	457.2
16	192	487.7
17	204	518.2
18	216	548.6
19	228	579.1
20	240	609.6